HAVE WE LEARNED ANYTHING YET?

Have We Learned Anything Yet?

A REFLECTION OF MANKIND'S HISTORY AND A HOPE OF WHAT'S TO COME

K. R. Hawthorne

k.r. publishing house

K. R. Publishing House

ISBN 978-1-7379826-0-9
Ebook ISBN 978-1-7379826-1-6
https://www.readkrhawthorne.com

Copyright © 2022 by K. R. Hawthorne

All rights reserved. No part of this book may be reproduced in any manner whatsoever without written permission except in the case of brief quotations embodied in critical articles and reviews.

K.R. Publishing House, 2022

Contents

Dedication	vi
Preface	3
1 How It Started and Where It's Going	6
2 Building a Legacy: The History of Mankind	18
3 War: What is it Good For?	43
4 History Repeats Itself	64
5 The Law of Truth	85
6 Eagles and Chickens: You are What You Believe	105
7 Have You Learned Anything Yet?	121
The Reader's Ending	126
Acknowledgements	134
REFERENCES	135
About K. R. Hawthorne	141

For the past, present, and future generations of mankind.

"Will this generation be able to turn things around and learn a valuable lesson from all of this? I hope so, but I have my doubts. The damage has been done. And as a lifelong student of history, it's quite evident that human beings don't learn from the mistakes of past generations."
— ***Aaron B. Powell, Voluntary***

"Your life is written in indelible ink. There's no going back to erase the past, tweak your mistakes, or fill in missed opportunities. When the moment's over, your fate is sealed.

But if you look closer, you notice the ink never really dries on any of our experiences. They can change their meaning the longer you look at them."
—***Klexo***

"There are ways of thinking about the past that aren't just nostalgia or regret. A kind of questioning that enriches an experience after the fact. To dwell on the past is to allow fresh context to trickle in over the years, and fill out the picture, to keep the memory alive and not just as a caricature of itself. So you can look fairly at a painful experience, and call it by its name.

Time is the most powerful force in the universe. It can turn a giant into someone utterly human, just trying to make their way through. Or tell you how you really felt about someone, even if you couldn't at the time. It can put your childhood dreams in context with adult burdens or turn a universal consensus into an embarrassing fad. It can expose cracks in a relationship that once seemed perfect. Or keep a friendship going by thoughts alone, even if you'll never see them again. It can flip your greatest shame into the source of your greatest power, or turn a jolt of pride into something petty, done for the wrong reasons, or make what felt like the end of the world look like a natural part of life.

The past is still mostly a blank page, so we may be doomed to repeat it. But it's still worth looking into if it brings you closer to the truth.

Maybe it's not so bad to dwell in the past, and muddle in the memories, to stem the simplification of time and put some craft back into it. Maybe we should think of memory itself as an art form in which the real work begins as soon as the paint hits the canvas. And remember that a work of art is never finished, only abandoned."

— ***The Dictionary of Obscure Sorrows***

Preface

If you're looking for a book of answers, this is surely not it. What I am attempting to present is questions we all might have, about certain circumstances of life that seem to repeat, not change or are slow to improve. My hope is that this book will cause you, the reader, to stir up a conversation of reflection with family, friends, colleagues, and strangers while also inspiring you to challenge your thinking and incite action on the world around you.

In all our doings and societal advances, have we truly learned anything yet about love, family, power, happiness, prosperity, leadership, or relationships? In mankind's 200,000 years of experience living on planet Earth, do we understand yet why we were created? Do we understand what we're supposed to do with our time here? And do we have a clue of how we should interact with the people and living things around us?

Well, we shall surely find out throughout our journey within the next few pages. Our journey will give us an opportunity to assess a variety of familiar and unfamiliar stories that are unique to our shared human history. Throughout this book, you will see sections labeled:

HAVE WE LEARNED ANYTHING YET?

When you see these sections, take time to consider the questions presented and discuss your beliefs and thoughts honestly with yourself and with someone close to you.

The Content of *Have We Learned Anything Yet?* reflects on the idea that humanity's progress has happened and hasn't happened. This book discusses difficult and remarkable stories that pertain to our shared human history. I also provide my personal account of pivotal moments that have shaped my thinking and the environment around me. *Have We Learned Anything Yet?* begins with my relationship with the question and progresses to stories of human history as it relates to the question. This is by no means to be a timeline of historical events. All the information presented is based on research and is proven factual. Throughout the book, I may simplify the word mankind for man; the word "man" is not single to the male gender. The word "man" includes both the male and female spirit.

Food for Thought

It is said that we can learn from our past. That each generation is wiser, makes smarter decisions, and improves the world. Maybe that's true; mankind has certainly evolved from its humble beginnings in caves to lavish palaces in Egypt, fortified Asian Dynasties, to the mighty Roman Empire, sophisticated diplomacy, and to the far-advanced Silicon Valley. Mankind has indeed always found a way to learn from our past and evolve in the preceding generations.

But isn't it also true that history repeats itself?

If we have truly learned from our past, why is it that we still have wars knowing the outcome is thousands of casualties and debt? Is fear the best method of persuasion? Are we still fascinated by the sight of fire? Why do we eat the extra slice of cake even though we know it's no good for us? Do you believe mankind is no better than the day of its creation? Can we ever attain perfection? Can we be on one accord to achieve higher results, maximum potential, and a harmonious coexistence?

Whatever you believe, I encourage you to continue reading and put life's biggest issues to the test. Ask the same question that I continue to ask...have we learned anything yet?

Now, I certainly do not want to give you the impression that I can answer the questions to life's most challenging issues or convey that I have all the answers. More truthfully, I have many questions and limited answers. No one today can fully grasp the why behind every moment in our ancestor's history. We can only speculate on what was and what could have been. This book aims for the future, the unknown, the unseen, and the unwritten. Can the arguments suggested in this book make the next generation better, and the generation after that, and the generation after that? History is made of events from the past, but history is also made of events planned for the future. Learn from the past, better today, and change tomorrow.

Ladies and Gentleman, I present to you...

Have We Learned Anything Yet?

1

How It Started and Where It's Going

An interesting question, isn't it?
Have we learned anything yet?

I remember the first time this question, have we learned anything yet, slipped into my mind. I was working on my undergraduate degree at Bowling Green State University and the question came to me during a lesson in one of my political science courses. Political science was not my major. I was taking the course as a general education class that was required by my university. The course was designed to expand my understanding of the United States government and its formation.

One day during class, a life-changing lesson made me question everything in my life. I questioned my government, religion, spirituality, and overall purpose in the world. As my professor continued through her lesson, I felt myself becoming uncomfortable and severely warm. In my chair, I was fidgety and began bouncing my right leg up and down repeatedly. I was burning with questions and looked around to see if anyone in the class of 250 students might be feeling like I was.

I received zero empathy from my peers. A quarter of the students were asleep, another quarter preoccupied with a conversation in their cellphones, and the other half diligently took notes while squinting at the slideshow presentation. I felt alone and perplexed. The class was coming to a close and the last thought on my mind was, have we learned anything yet?

You might be wondering, what was this life-changing lesson? What could have me so fidgety that I could barely contain myself? My professor had just dropped a bombshell on me, and I was left sitting there picking up my jaw and the fragile pieces of my life off the floor.

We were learning about the various events that shaped the formation of the United States. I learned that in the early discussions of the constitution, slavery was deeply considered for abolishment. Benjamin Franklin spoke on the matter in numerous essays and meetings.

In his essay, "An Address to the Public," Franklin warned of the effects slavery has on a man:

> "The unhappy man, who has long been treated as a brute animal, too frequently sinks beneath the common standard of the human species. The galling chains that bind his body also fetter his intellectual faculties and impair the social affections of his heart. Accustomed to moving like a mere machine, by the will of a master, reflection is suspended; he has not the power of choice, and reason and conscience have but little influence over his conduct, because he is chiefly governed by the passion of fear. He is poor and friendless, perhaps worn out by extreme labour, age, and disease. Under such circumstances, freedom may often prove a misfortune to himself and prejudicial to

society. Attention to emancipated black people, it is, therefore, to be hoped, will become a branch of our national policy."

Franklin simply stated that a human reduced to operating in a machine-like fashion would lose his identity. That person will lose the power to choose for themselves. Common sense and reason will not be found in their abilities. Being controlled by fear, this person will end up poor, friendless, worn out, and diseased. This essay was written in 1789.

How could the advice of one of America's forefathers fall on deaf ears? Why did the public not adhere to it? The presiding government officials turned their heads to it, ignored his advice, and life went on. For close to 100 more years, life went on. In the end, the industry won, a compromise was made, and all who opposed slavery reluctantly looked in the other direction. They made a little murmur from time to time, but the change was slow and met with a constant rebellion.

In 1865, the physical chains were unclamped from the ankles of the "unhappy man", but the "unhappy man" still remembers the chains and behaves like he is still in bondage. And the chain master knowing this pulls on the invisible chains from time to time to assert his perceived power.

HAVE WE LEARNED ANYTHING YET?

What the founding fathers hoped to achieve in America was a place where all were welcomed and would work together to do what was profitable for the nation. I believe Benjamin Franklin believed that educating and relinquishing ownership of Black people was a part of the promise of the United States. How long will it take for the rest of society to believe the same? What is so jarring about a Black person's skin color or physical attributes that make them the center of inequality and discrimination to this day?

To this day, we still have Americans that are descendants of slavery who have been subject to generational poverty, poor education, sickness, and loss of identity due to their many years of oppression. As Franklin stated, when a person loses their identity, they fall victim to just about anything. Blown away by this information, I received a new revelation. I began to dive further into history and discover the patterns, causes, and effects of historical events and the question kept coming to me...have we learned anything yet?

I was overwhelmed by the question, maybe slightly obsessed!

I began to view life from a new lens. Conversations easily led me to question why? Why was this, this way and that, that way? Why couldn't this be that way and that be this way? An everyday task that was once routine, I began to question how this had been done before, what the outcome was, and how have we improved on that idea. Is there a better way?

Whenever I see a homeless person or a family living in poverty, it brings me back to that question.

HAVE WE LEARNED ANYTHING YET?

How do we have trees that produce food naturally and people are still hungry? How are we able to print money but not able to eradicate poverty? At what point do people give up on people and stop caring? In a world of infinite opportunity, why does it appear that some people are deprived of these opportunities?

What are we missing? What have we lost? What have we forgotten?

Every day there are countless situations I can apply the question to. Situations such as race relations, interpersonal relationships, media influence, educational systems, foreign and political affairs, child-rearing, and leadership.

In small group circles and houses all over the world, people are discussing why this nation bombed that nation. Why did this man die because of his skin color? How come our children are lazy and lack the morals our parents had? How come mainstream music does not have any meaning or substance? Why is mainstream news coverage always negative and depressing? Why didn't my elected official keep his campaign promises?

We complain about these things, discuss them, and even debate them. But change is slow, if at all. We see all the bad, and have ideas for improvement but more or less keep the status quo the same. Why are we humans persistent in complaining but not changing?

Life is like a person driving around a racetrack. Each turn has its own challenges. Some turns will curve up the wall causing the driver to make an adjustment so as not to go over the wall. Other turns are constructed to come quick and are sharp, shaped like a V. The sharp turns require the driver to proceed with caution, press the brake, and get to the inside of the turn.

Then there is this final turn that is an illusion and is displayed as a wall. To master this turn, you must let go of reason and drive through the wall. Our intellect tells us we can see a wall. We understand that we are speeding closer to it. And our knowledge of walls reminds us that if we do not slow down and make a decision to press the brake, we will crash. Your coach tells you to trust that you will not crash and that the wall is an illusion. And yet, with all this information, intellect, and ability, when you reach the wall, you brake hard and come to a screeching halt.

Why?

Is it because in the back of our minds, we believe we know something different than the other guy? The "I am smarter than" or "That's not how things are done" mentality? Or is it something else entirely that prevents us from having the courage to face what's beyond the wall?

Well, I am here to tell you that history is our coach and if we listen to the lessons written therein, we can do more than we ever thought was possible. Each person's action or lack of action affects one another. Every person who contributes something significant to the world pushes us forward. Every person who told a kid it was okay to dream contributed to society. Every time a person dies prematurely, we are set back; for that was an idea that was not manifested, an interaction that would not change someone else's life.

* * *

A few years back, I was shopping at my local grocery store and there was a woman ahead of me in line. She was juggling two jugs of milk, baby medicine, and a few other odds and ends. Seeing the woman in distress, I offered her space in my shopping cart. She was so thankful and quickly filled my top basket with her items. As the self-checkout line was getting shorter and we were moving closer to the front of the line, a demanding thought in my mind said, "Pay for her groceries."

I instantly combated that thought with, "Pshhhttt why? I'm sure this woman has enough money to buy her own groceries. Plus, I don't want to offend her." I continued to wrestle with this thought for about a minute or so until I finally said to myself, "Well... maybe...ok. Let's just see how it goes."

It was time for us to part ways and she gathered her items and went to her mini register. My boyfriend (now husband) and I went to our mini register. I kept hearing that thought in my mind to "Pay for her groceries." But I kept reasoning and continued checking out.

As we were scanning our last item, there was an issue with the barcode. We kept scanning the item and nothing was registering. We flagged the attendant down for assistance and as the attendant was coming toward us, I glanced over at the woman. I saw her bagging her last item and reaching into her purse to grab her credit card. She swiped her card and selfishly I thought, "Well, I'm in the clear now."

I turned back to my register, where the attendant was helping us key in our trouble-making barcode. I look back over to the woman and saw her swiping her card again. I can see something is going wrong and her card is not working. At that moment, the woman turns and looks me directly in the eyes; the look she gave me confirmed my prognosis. For a moment, I was frozen and it was as if she knew what I was thinking and tussling with inside my mind. Her eyes talked back to me and said, "Yes, I need your help."

Instead of walking over and swiping my card on her register, which by the way was my first thought, I told the attendant helping us to go over to her. After helping us, he went to her mini register and brought her and her items up to the attendant's station. He must have thought something was wrong with her mini-register. She swiped her card again and still had the same problem. She then digs through her purse and pockets, searching for paper bills and coins to pay for her groceries.

At this point, you're probably thinking, "Surely now I would act and pay for the woman's groceries!" But I am ashamed to say even still, I did not move. The woman miraculously came up with the money she needed to pay for her own groceries. She grabbed her bags and went her way and we grabbed our bags and went ours.

Why did I tell you this story? It's like I stated previously; one person's actions or lack of action affects us all. What if that was all the money that woman had left in the world? What if she needed that cash to pay off a debt? What if she was having a rough day and a simple act of kindness could have saved her from a destructive act? Extreme maybe, but possible.

Her groceries were no more than $30, and I would not have been out of money by paying for her groceries. In fact, I could have paid for that 100 times over. My selfish act had a ripple effect; the same is true for all of you reading this. My sincerest apologies to that woman, her family, and all impacted.

We all have a responsibility in this world to leave it better than we found it; that happens day by day in small acts. Changing the world seems so large, far-fetched, and a dream to most, but it's simpler than we think.

ACT II

The second and more pressing time I was inspired to write on this subject was after I began reading the Bible. I chose to read the Bible after I recommitted my life to Christ and in doing so, I wanted to learn more about the faith that I was choosing to believe in.

I was fascinated by the stories that I read in the Bible, such as the story of Moses taking on Pharaoh to free the enslaved Jewish citizens or Mighty King David conquering every nation he stood against while singing and praising God with veracity. Some of my favorite lessons occurred while reading the miraculous acts performed by Jesus. Such as when he healed the blind man and fed the multitudes. But more than anything, I was intrigued by the stories that I could relate to in my lifetime, like the story of the prodigal son.

In the story of the prodigal son, Jesus tells a tale about a man who had two sons. The younger son, once he reached the proper age, asked his father for his share of his father's estate. So the father agreed and divided the estate between his two sons.

Not long after the father gave his sons their portion, the younger son gathered all his belongings and set off into a new land. The older brother chose to stay on the family farm and helped his parents with the family business.

Meanwhile, the younger brother lived wild, lavishly, and loosely with his finances and eventually squandered all his wealth within a short timeframe. His misfortune was sure to increase. Not only was he out of money in a foreign country, but now the country he was in was experiencing a famine. Hungry and without any money, he began to be in need. In the act of desperation, he went and searched for work. He eventually found a countryman who offered him lodging and paid work.

This citizen was a farmer and hired the young man to attend to his pigs. The young man was immediately sent to the fields to feed the pigs. The farmer had many fat pigs and the young man could see that they were well fed.

The young man longed to fill his stomach with anything. His stomach was annoyingly reminding him that it had been days since it had last received any substance. The smothered corn cobs and chunky food scraps the pigs were eating began to look increasingly better.

He began to think to himself, "I've not eaten in days; surely the farmer won't notice if I only take but a handful of the pigs' dinner."

The growling became unbearable and his flesh began to weaken. He looked around and saw no one looking, so he humbled himself and dipped his frail fingers into the pig's trough for a scoop. He scooped himself out a large handful of the pigs' chunky slop. He slowly raised his hands to his mouth and began to bend his face towards his unfortunate meal. As he was about to swallow his slimy, chunky slop, he suddenly came to his senses.

He spat out the slop and said to himself, "How many of my father's hired servants have food to spare, and here I am starving to death! I will return to my father and say to him: Father, I have sinned against heaven and you. I am no longer worthy of being called your son; make me like one of your hired servants."

With that in mind, he got up from the muck he was in, dropped his slop where he stood, and went to his father, leaving the pigs to enjoy the rest of their dinner.

As the young man was coming down the road, his father, who was working in the yard, saw him and became filled with compassion for his returning son. He ran to his son, threw his arms around him, and kissed him!

The son said to him, 'Father, I have sinned against heaven and you. I am no longer worthy of being called your son."

His father disregarded his statement and said to his servants, "Quick! Bring the best robe and put it on him. Put a ring on his finger and sandals on his feet. Bring the fattest calf and kill it. Let's have a feast and celebrate! For this son of mine was thought dead and is alive again; he was lost and is found!"

And So they began to celebrate.

Meanwhile, the older son was still working in the field. When he came near the house, he heard music and dancing. So he called one of the servants and asked what was happening.

The servant replied, "Your brother has come back home and your father has killed the fattest calf and called for celebration because he has his young son back safe and sound."

The older brother became furious and refused to go inside to the party. His father went out and pleaded with him to join the party.

But he answered his father, "Look, Father! I've been slaving for you all these years and never disobeyed your orders. Yet you never gave me even a young goat so I could celebrate with my friends. But when this son of yours who has squandered your property with prostitutes comes home, you kill the fattest calf for him!'

"My son," the father said, "you are always with me, and everything I have is yours. But we must celebrate and be merry because your brother, my son, was dead and is alive again; he was lost and was found."

I believe the younger son learned a lesson in frugality and living sensibly. I believe he also learned that timing is everything. As a young person, you may be eager to grow up and become an adult to take on adult-like responsibilities as soon as you turn eighteen. However, it is wise not to rush leaving home before you've had the opportunity to learn valuable skills to ensure your success in the adult world.

I am convinced, that the older brother learned the biggest lesson. He was so caught up in pleasing his father and being the better son that it drove him to envy. He was envious that his brother received his inheritance early. He was envious that his brother had moved away from home, partied, and lived a whole new life. He was envious that his father accepted his younger brother back home after all he did. His envy blocked him from realizing that if his younger brother could ask for his inheritance and leave home, why wouldn't he be able to gather his inheritance, leave home, and start a new life as well?

HAVE WE LEARNED ANYTHING YET?

How many young people can relate to that story? How many times have you disappointed your parents only to find them lovingly forgiving you and welcoming you back with open arms? Or are you the older brother? Have you ever felt overshadowed by someone? Did you know that you always had the power to change your circumstance?

How could these same feelings or situations that occurred 2,000 years ago possibly still have relevance in this day and age? Have we not become smarter? Do people truly repeat the same behavior time after time? Century after century?

Do we have innate characteristics that stay with us from generation to generation? Characteristics that no matter how advanced we think our society or way of thinking has become can be traced back to the beginning days of man.

History is our teacher, our coach, and a reminder of what was and what can be. We must learn from history if we hope to improve in the future. History erased is lessons forgotten and time wasted for the future; the keys to our future are breadcrumbed in the past. It is every human's responsibility to be seekers of history's wisdom and present action-takers to produce a future worth living in.

2

Building a Legacy: The History of Mankind

Go back to the earliest days of mankind, when we were at the grassroots of learning about the world around us—a time when civilizations consisted of no more than twenty or so parents, siblings, and cousins. Our ancestors had to discover ways to keep order and protect their tribe. To establish order, our ancestors created roles and social hierarchies to set rules and provide structure. Typically in this ecosystem, Elders were tasked with the important job of leading the people in wisdom and judgment. Young and able men became hunters and defenders of the tribe. Women became producers and focused on growing crops, making garments, and tending to the children. And lastly, to progress and lead the tribe forward, a single individual was deemed chief, king, or leader.

To have any sustaining tribe, growth in agriculture is essential to the development and longevity of the civilization. Production of crops such as corn, wheat, beans, and rice is vital to feeding and sustaining the tribe. Cattle and animals were bred to assist with daily work, feed the family, or sold to bring wealth. And for a while, all is well. History showed us when societies became increasingly complex and populations grew to the thousands, this tribal village system eventually would need to evolve.

Combine an increasing population with sophisticated hand tools plus the need for advanced weaponry and the result will be a shift in the type of work needed by the society. Advancements in infrastructure and habitat dwellings would now need to be considered. To build more advanced infrastructure for the town, leaders would seek people that were skilled in building such as carpenters, blacksmiths, and masons. Well-educated individuals or scholars would find work as scribes, priests, and bureaucrats. Their job was to think of ideas and philosophies that the society would live by. Some agriculture producers may even shift from life in the fields to life in the town. Those who didn't could benefit by producing a surplus of crops that they might sell in the town market.

With this type of growth comes new issues that the elders may not have seen before or have any knowledge of. Issues such as:

Is it lawful to marry your brother's widow? Is it a bad sign if your hair falls out? What god do we pray to? Should we pay a tax to the King? How do we treat foreigners?

Counsel and judgments from the elders can often be inconsistent, contradictory, corrupt, misleading, and not based on any truth. This can cause much confusion in this new and growing land. Different cultures have faced the challenge of leading their growing nation with various solutions. When elder counsel was no longer suitable, many societies turned to creating and establishing a set of rules, laws, or codes of conduct to provide consistency in wisdom and punishment for its citizens.

Divine Law or Religious Law was one of the first codes of conduct put in place to govern large bodies of people. Religious texts like the Tanakh, Quran, Bible, Sutras, and Vedas outline divine laws and tell the stories of our ancient ancestors who did acts of kindness, miracles, destruction, and evil. The stories in each of those religious texts are purposed to provide examples of how to live right by the standard of The Creator and give wisdom to their believers.

The Law presented by Moses, also known as Mosaic Law, is one of humanity's founding governing laws from the God of Israel meant to establish order and protect citizens from the consequences of bad behavior. An infraction of Mosaic Law was different from any other laws at the time because disobedience to these laws was not only an infraction on mankind, but also was seen as disobedience to God's will and could result in a punishment from God. Mosaic Law begins with the Ten Commandments (see Table 1) that provide the foundation of moral rules that God expects his children to follow.

According to the Torah in Jewish culture and The Old Testament in the Christian Bible, there are 613 other laws that God instructed Moses to write to give more details on behavior and punishments for various day-to-day issues. The laws written through Moses have guided many nations for centuries. In some cases, when a society is fully persuaded to follow Divine Law, a reduction in major crimes can be seen. Studies have supported that in areas with a high religious following, the area notices a reduction in murder, suicide, and theft.[3]

HAVE WE LEARNED ANYTHING YET?

Many growing nations have been faced with a similar challenge of learning how to lead a large body of people. What do you think? *How does a good leader meet the ever-changing needs of the people? How do you use good judgment to lead people? How does a good leader keep order in growing chaos? In what ways can corruption be eliminated? Can Divine Law be the only necessary way to lead people due to the moral implications of following God's* word? Is punishment necessary for disobedience? Who is the most important class of citizens in a Kingdom?

Table 1

The Ten Commandments	
I. I am the LORD your God, who brought you out of the land of Egypt where you were slaves. You must not have any other gods except me	II. You must not make for yourselves an idol that looks like anything in the sky above or on the earth below
III. You must not use the name of the LORD your God in vain	IV. Remember the sabbath day, to keep it holy
V. Honour your father and your mother	VI. You shall not kill.
VII. You shall not commit adultery	VIII. You shall not steal
IX. You shall not bear false witness against your neighbor	X. You shall not covet your neighbor's house; you shall not covet your neighbor's wife, nor anything that is your neighbor's.

Mesopotamia (mainly modern-day Iraq and Kuwait) is often referred to as the cradle of civilization because some of the most influential early city-states and empires first emerged there. Associated with Mesopotamia are ancient cultures like the Sumerians, Assyrians, Akkadians, and the Babylonians. One of the most notable of the mentioned civilizations is the Babylonian Kingdom. The Babylonian Kingdom is a great example of what it takes to grow a nation from humble beginnings into a massive empire.

Prior to the reign of King Hammurabi (1894 BC), the Babylonian Kingdom consisted of only four small city-states for about 100 years. During Hammurabi's reign, he expanded the empire to eventually control all of ancient Mesopotamia, which covered more than fifteen villages and major city-states. He began his reign by centralizing and streamlining his administration. He also continued his father's building projects to enlarge and heighten the walls of the city in hopes of fortifying the capital from all invaders. He paid careful attention to the needs of the people and improved the irrigation system for the fields, and provided maintenance to the infrastructures of the cities under his control.[4] Hammurabi freed Babylon from foreign rule and then conquered the whole southern Mesopotamia region. This brought stability and the name of Babylon throughout the region. The Babylonian Kingdom went on to be one of the wealthiest nations of their time.

Much of King Hammurabi's success can be attributed to a compilation of laws called the Code of Hammurabi. The Code of Hammurabi written around 1754 BC, combined and improved upon the earlier written laws of Sumer, Akkad, and Assyria. Hammurabi's code is one of the oldest deciphered writings of significant length in the world. The Code was written on stone slabs and clay tablets and consists of 282 laws with scaled punishments depending on social status.

The famous saying "An eye for an eye, a tooth for a tooth" can be traced back to the Code of Hammurabi. Hammurabi was wise in that he improved on the laws of the leaders before him. He was able to lead his people into a new era and provided a system of order that kept citizens accountable. This form of order and governance has evolved many times throughout history and if laws are enforced appropriately, the society thrives. Can this type of law and order society still thrive in a nation when the population reaches the millions?

Hammurabi's influence on law and order can be seen in the succeeding generations as they further developed his laws and societies became more complex. Many of those same laws can be seen in modern law today. Table 2 compares the Hammurabi Code, the Law of Moses, and the las in the United States.

Table 2.

Hammurabi Code	Law of Moses	United States Laws
#1: If a man brings an accusation against a man, and charges him with a crime, but cannot prove it, he, the accuser shall be put to death.	Deuteronomy 19:19 (NIV)Then do to the false witness as that witness intended to do to the other party. You must purge the evil from among you.	Defamation is the action of damaging the good reputation of someone. In the case of defamation, a lawsuit can be filed, and the person accused can be fined or serve jail time.

#22: If anyone is committing a robbery and is caught, then he shall be put to death.	Exodus 20:1 (KJV) Thou shall not steal	Someone guilty of theft can pay a fine or serve jail time, usually depending on the value of the item(s) taken.
#196: If a man destroys the eye of another man, they shall destroy his eye.	Exodus 21:25 (BSB) But if a serious injury results, then you must require a life for a life, an eye for eye, tooth for tooth, hand for hand, foot for foot, burn for burn, wound for wound, and stripe for stripe.	A person committing assault (physically injuring someone else) will be arrested and taken to court. They will likely serve jail time.
#195: If a son strikes his father, they shall cut off his fingers.	Exodus 20: 12 (NIV) Honor your father and your mother, so that you may live long in the land the Lord your God is giving you.	A person commits domestic violence by intentionally causing or attempting to cause bodily injury to a member of the victim's family or household.

GOVERNING THE WORLD

Through military advances, some nations were able to extend their rulership to vast areas of the globe and millions of individuals. Two of the earliest empires to conquer many nations and have large populations were the Roman Empire (27 BC - 476 AD) and The Han Dynasty of China (202 BC - 220 AD). The Roman Empire lasted over 1,000 years and the Han Dynasty reigned for around 500 years. In regards to population, at the height of both the Roman Empire and the Han Dynasty, each had populations of about 60-65 million people, housing about a quarter of the world's population.[5]

So how did the Roman Empire and Han Dynasty maintain control over their societies and massive populations over a large geographical area? The Roman Empire's long-lasting success is attributed to its military occupation and democratic government. The Han dynasty's legacy is attributed to the cultural influence of Confucianism and their empire's commitment to virtues and the arts. We can learn a great deal from studying both empires.

The rulers of these great empires had only a handful of successful empires to emulate and did not have sophisticated technology that allowed them to communicate quickly with their extended subjects. So how were they able to rule for so long and have a lasting impact on the world around them? *Let's dive deep and see what we can discover!*

Many aspects of modern society have been influenced by the 1,000-year reign of the Roman Empire. From the spread of Christianity to the creation of Roman law, the development of democratic government practices, influences in language, literature, art, infrastructure, and city planning are all areas where the influences of roman ideas can be seen. Roman influences have had considerable importance in law and gave most of Europe a foundation of legal ideas and legal rules.

Prior to Roman Law, many nations relied on customs and traditions as laws. It was not until the Twelves Tables were introduced that Europe would have a common inventory of legal ideas, a common grammar of legal thought, and, to a varying but considerable extent, a common mass of legal rules[6].

Some of the laws from the Twelve Tables include[7]:

Table 3.

Laws of the Twelve Tables	
As a man has provided in his will in regard to his money and the care of his property, so let it be binding. If he has no heir and dies intestate (without a written will), let the nearest agnate (male descendant) have the inheritance.	If one shall permit himself to be summoned as a witness, or has been a weigher, if he does not give his testimony, let him be noted as dishonest and incapable of acting again as witness.
If one is slain while committing theft by night, he is rightly slain.	If one is mad but has no guardian, the power over him and his money shall belong to his agnates and the members of his gens.

It is unlawful for a thief to be killed by day....unless he defends himself with a weapon; even though he has come with a weapon, unless he shall use the weapon and fight back, you shall not kill him. And even if he resists, first call out so that someone may hear and come up.

Any person who destroys by burning any building or heap of corn deposited alongside a house shall be bound, scourged, and put to death by burning at the stake provided that he has committed the said misdeed with malice aforethought; but if he shall have committed it by accident, that is, by negligence, it is ordained that he repair the damage or, if he be too poor to be competent for such punishment, he shall receive a lighter punishment.

Should a tree on a neighbor's farm be bent crooked by the wind and lean over your farm, you may take legal action for removal of that tree.

A child born after ten months since the father's death will not be admitted into a legal inheritance.

A man might gather up fruit that was falling down onto another man's farm.

The women shall not tear their faces nor wail on account of the funeral.

Most of the laws written in Table 3 are moral laws and deal with particular situations that we may say today are common sense or conditionally based on the situation. However, when building a society, these rudimentary laws were necessary to provide a common code of right and wrong. If these laws were not written, people would act based on their needs and not in regards to the overall well-being of the society.

Say for example, if I am hungry and I see fruit on a tree, I may decide to snatch the fruit from the tree and eat it without any regard to whose tree it is. A law had to be put in place to prevent people from walking into your yard and taking fruit from your tree without asking. This may sound silly to us today, but in ancient times this was a serious matter that someone could kill you over.

Without law, this act may be deemed right in the eyes of the eater, but not right in the eyes of the planter. Law was created to mediate these situations so all people in society would know how to conduct themselves. Laws were created to maintain order and give people a sense of right and wrong in pursuit to protect people from each other.

We can see the influence of some of these laws in modern society. In Roman Law, a deceased person's last will and testament for their inheritance, if written, was a legally binding document and must be carried out as written by the deceased. This practice is still occurring today.

Another practice that can be traced to Roman Law is the honesty of a witness in a court trial. In the United States, anyone called to be a witness in a court of law is held to a high standard. If they are found to have provided a dishonest testimony on the witness stand, they are subject to hefty fines and potentially time in prison.

Written laws also allow a leader to lead more efficiently across a large body of people when the majority of their subjects know what is acceptable and unacceptable behavior in the absence of leadership. A written law and subsequently the consequences for violating that law can be carried out by anyone that is appointed to judge that case without involving the King or Queen. By having written laws, a leader is able to lead large bodies of people without ever leaving the palace.

HAVE WE LEARNED ANYTHING YET?

It appears that we may have learned that our ancestor's laws had meaning and were useful. Do you believe laws protect people or do you believe common sense should rule?

> ### ROMAN LAW
>
> Later in humanity's evolution, more specific laws were created to justify and categorize the complexity of human actions. The idea to identify, classify, and deem what is a given right to a particular citizen dates back to the founding days of Roman law. In those days (753–731 BC), it was known as jus civile (civil law). Jus civile was based on custom and legislation; it applied exclusively to Roman citizens. Foreigners had no rights and, unless protected by some treaty between their state and Rome, they could be seized like property by any Roman citizen.[8]
>
> Most of Rome's constitution was an unwritten set of guidelines and principles passed down mainly through tradition, custom, and learned experiences. Checks and balances, the separation of powers, vetoes, filibusters, quorum requirements, term limits, impeachments, the powers of the purse, and regularly scheduled elections are all concepts that originated in the Roman constitution. Even some lesser-used modern constitutional concepts, such as the block voting found in the electoral college of the United States, originate from ideas found in the Roman written and unwritten constitution.[9]

BUILDING A LEGACY

The Han Dynasty was much like the Roman Empire in size and population. The Han Dynasty experienced many leaders and flourished in culture, arts, mathematics, and science throughout its 500-year reign. The founder of the Han, formally known as Emperor Gaozu, was born Liu Bang and grew up as a commoner coming from a peasant family[10]. As an adult, he became a low-level official in the Qin army. He later became an outlaw and would lead a revolt against the Qin Empire. After more than three years of fighting, Bang was the leader of a large army. He defeated many Kings in war to become emperor of China.

As the new emperor, Liu Bang (202 BC - 195 BC) inherited a large empire and the foundation of the imperial rule laid by the Qin court. He took careful steps to make sure he would not make the same mistake as the dynasty he overthrew. As a former commoner, he understood the life of peasantry and initiated programs, such as lowering taxes and opening up bureaucratic positions to all classes, to provide people with upward mobility. He utilized a standardized written language for the whole empire and made a focus to promote Confucianism throughout the kingdom.

One of Bang's predecessors Wu the Great (141 BC - 87 BC), would add to his legacy and be known for his expansionist policies and reforms. His early reforms opened up possibilities for the lower class that had never existed before in governmental positions. He curtailed the greed of the nobles and expanded the law code so that all were equal under the law.

Wu also expanded trade with countries in the west, and soon, foreigners brought wealth plus new technologies and ideas to the empire. Through trade on the Silk Road, The Han people's knowledge of the outside world, philosophy and religion, and technology increased. Skilled workers made advances in refining iron and making steel weapons and tools during and after his reign. So by the creation of wealth, territorial expansion, and strength, the Han empire began to prosper[10].

The Han Dynasty, unlike the Romans, relied mostly on free labor rather than slaves for growth in agriculture. Instead of using slave labor, Chinese landowners would use contracts and money to strike bargains with laborers. In modern times this would look like an employer posting a job and a person seeking work agreeing to do the job in exchange for money and a binding contract of the terms of work. The free farmers were largely self-sufficient and did not rely on government intervention. The farmers would produce goods in demand for their village or town.

Chinese emperors and their officials were keenly aware of the importance of the agricultural economy. A flourishing and well-managed agriculture meant satisfied people and a large surplus. A weak and poorly managed agricultural economy harmed not only the people but also the emperor and his government.[11]

Han farmers were supposed to grow enough food for their own families as well as help stock the shared storehouses. The surplus was used to support its rulers, bureaucrats, and armies and enable it to offer famine relief from stored grain supplies when necessary. Civilians were also expected to provide the government with one month of free labor to build canals and roads.

After Wu, the next several emperors would come into power as children or teens and unfortunately die young on the throne. Power was then consistently transferred to their maternal uncles in the role of commander in chief. The people started being unfairly treated and corruption was at an all-time high. That was until one of the last notable emperors of the Han Dynasty; Emperor Wang Mang, took the throne (9 AD - 23 AD).

He was a bit of a radical idealist who, when he took power, broke with tradition and declared *The New Dynasty* had come! Mang broke apart the aristocratic estates and redistributed them among the peasants. Mang changed society by fully abolishing slavery, redistributing the land, and issuing a new currency[10]. Unfortunately, the good times were not here to stay as a natural disaster caused massive flooding. The peasant class became frustrated by the massive flooding and by 23 AD, their anger manifested into a rebel group called the Red Eyebrows. The Red Eyebrows would lead a revolt against Mang and soon after, he was killed.[10]

This action resulted in a downward spiral of the great dynasty. During the last two decades, there were a lot of assassinations in the imperial court. In 194 AD, there was a great famine due to a plague of locusts. The empire faced numerous attacks and rebellions and, by 220 AD would be dissolved and broken up.

Although their downfall wasn't pretty, we owe a lot to the Han Dynasty, such as advances in science and technology like the invention of paper and the wheelbarrow. Plus advances in anesthesiology, mathematics, and astronomy. Their focus on shared labor and resources allowed the people to maintain their way of life while contributing to society. We can also learn the effects of great leadership, corruption, and the importance of the people's voice.

Happy subjects resulted in a prosperous kingdom. Great leaders like Bang and Wu considered the livelihood of their people. This allowed for them to have loyal citizens and a prosperous reign. In the case of Mang, although he had good intentions and big ideas for the country, he could not control the weather. Sometimes in life, our plans do not always go forth as we hoped they would. The corrupt leaders of the Han Dynasty ultimately led to the Dynasty's downfall. Their unfair policies and deception led to turmoil and division. History shows us that when leaders put the needs of a few over the needs of the many, it sows mistrust and a rebellion of the people is inevitable.

HAVE WE LEARNED ANYTHING YET?

The Wu Dynasty is not the only society that was brought down by corrupt individuals, can you think of any other societies ancient or modern that struggled with corruption? What is at the root of corruption and how do we put an end to it?

CIVILIAN RIGHTS: EUROPEAN DOMINATION

Civilian rights are an idea that has been tested and viewed differently by every nation everywhere throughout history. From the beginning of mankind, leaders had to decide what was allowed within their environment, what justice looks like, and what punishments are necessary for disorderly conduct.

Fast forward to 1492, when European exploration took off; although Europe represented only about eight percent of the planet's landmass, from 1492 to 1914, Europeans (mainly Britain and Spain) conquered or colonized more than eighty percent of the entire world. They were firm in their beliefs that European living is God-mandated and tribal living is savagery. Nearly 400 years of European domination over most of the globe has led to lingering inequality and long-lasting effects in many formerly colonized countries, including poverty and slow economic growth. The effect of European domination has impacted continents such as Australia, Africa, Asia, India, North America, and South America.

In a study of the Psychological Stages of Colonialism, Hussein A. Bulhan paints an excellent picture of the outcomes and lasting impacts of European colonization in Africa:

> "The distinction of races and associated claim of natural superiority enabled Europeans to carry out three cataclysmic assaults using maximum violence (including genocide) that later became global. The first

assault was on the world of things, particularly the land of conquered non-European peoples, to exploit gold, silver, and other commodities. The second assault was on the world of people for obtaining free labor and carrying out sexual exploitation. The third assault was the world of meaning by changing indigenous religions, knowledge, and identities."[12]

Many African nations were under European rule up until the very recent 1960s. The outcome of generations of oppression and forcefulness to adopt European culture has left the entire continent at a loss of historical identity.

Bulhan continues, "The colonization of America subsequently fueled the capture, transport, and enslavement of Africans in the Americas and the Caribbean. The Atlantic Slave Trade represents the largest importation of slaves in the history of the world. This trade not only caused immense suffering for persons forced into slavery but also enabled Europeans to expand their settlement in the New World and earn substantial capital for Europeans to finance the industrial revolution.[12]

At least three outcomes of slavery seem certain. Firstly, slavery pauperized and depopulated the African continent, stealing its young and productive members and derailing the political history and economic development of its people. Secondly, this system of slavery consolidated the dominant-dominated relations between Europeans and non-Europeans, making ethnic superiority the primary justification for colonial exploitation that continues to the present in different guises. Thirdly, Europeans and their descendants reaped more than economic benefits from slavery. Fed better, their population increased. With new wealth and industry, they developed better technology to further conquer and exploit others[13].

Slavery ended when it was no longer economically or politically productive. Yet the European pursuit of profit, racism, and self-aggrandizement did not end. Instead, it grew more with the development of industries that required more raw materials, more cheap or free labor, and more markets for manufactured goods[14].

Due to the lost contest over the definition and naming of reality, the experience and story of the colonized await documenting and telling. Not hearing or reading about either, people assume they do not exist. The forgotten or distorted past leaves the colonized in a state of ignorance and confusion, with no lessons learned to understand the present or chart a new future. Colonialism today is more entrenched objectively and subjectively than in the past."

The end of The Civil War officially abolished slavery in the United States, but it didn't end discrimination against the descendants of slaves. Descendants of slaves continued to endure devastating effects of racism, inequality, and prejudice especially in the southern states of America for centuries. African nations that gained independence after generations of European colonization believed they would experience a time of freedom and prosperity. Sadly this was not so.

Legislation can put on paper a person's God-given rights, but the mindset of man also has to be fully persuaded and agree with the legislative decision. If the mindset does not change, people on both sides will quickly resort to their previous behaviors and beliefs and life will continue to go on.

History is always written by the winners. If we are to do better as a human race, we must address the lingering effects of European colonization on humanity. We must look at life from the lens of humankind and not as individual nations or races. We must come to terms that the world we enjoy today was largely built on the suffering of people with brown flesh. We must also come to terms that the ideas of white flesh individuals largely influenced the world we enjoy today. However, flesh color does not determine inferiority or superiority. Flesh color determines nothing.

So, how do we attain peace, understanding, and forgiveness?

I believe it is important to write your own history. Even if you believe that you have not done anything of significance yet. History is merely a compilation of people's stories, experiences, failures, and triumphs. Each story is important because it weaves all of humanity's stories together. When we take an aerial eye view of our lives, we can see the stitches connecting all of us. We can see where we got our humanistic nature, behaviors, and attitudes.

When we write our stories down, we give the future generations the opportunity to see life from our perspective. This gives our descendants an opportunity to do the same and even better than the generation before them. It is our duty to write our stories and pass them down. If we fail to record our stories, experiences, and failures in our own history, our children may never fully understand who they are. Our children will be taught history from other people's perspectives and values. A wise parent includes their money and their own recorded history into their children's inheritance.

The stories of the oppressed must be told. Written history tells the story of the conquerors. The beliefs, traditions, and customs of the oppressed have been erased, burned, and reprogrammed. It's time for the dry bones to speak once again and tell a new tale for all of us to hear and learn from.

Symbolism Text vs. Written Word

The early humans of the world discovered how to bring forth fire from everyday objects, and they used that fire to keep their families warm and provide meals. From those experiences, our ancestors shared their knowledge with the next generation through storytelling. When storytelling was no longer sufficient, man was given the idea to carve their stories and tradition in stone, animal fats, and later papyrus scrolls. This would ensure that they would always be remembered and immortalized throughout history. Thanks to these written stories, we today can study and speculate on what was and tell their stories from a new era perspective.

The Egyptians and Mayans used hieroglyphics, the Ancient Chinese wrote in ox and turtle bones, and modern society uses a combination of letters and pictures such as emoji's to tell our story. See Figure 1 to see how pictorial writing has evolved over the centuries.

There are prevalent limits on what you can say with pictures. The written word is infinitely more adaptable. It is believed that's why Greece rather than Egypt leapt forward and why Shakespeare was more articulate than the Aztecs. In an article written by Jonathan Jones of the Guardian, Jones states, "Ancient American civilizations that used visual symbols as a way to express language were oddly similar to Egypt in their mixture of expression. The Maya carved beautiful language icons yet never developed metalwork, let alone tragic drama. There is strong evidence that the abstract written word is essential to advance ideas, poetry and argument to their highest levels"[15]

Imagine describing a rose with an emoji. There are limits to what you would be able to articulate, such as the dangerous beauty of a rose or the aroma that it exudes when in bloom. It would be difficult to describe all of the characteristics of a thorne and how it bows outward and up to the sky as it matures. One would not fully grasp or even comprehend the beauty of the petals as light refracts and brings forth the shades of red on each and every last petal. The development of written language allowed for sophisticated thought transfer that aligned more accurately to your thinking than a picture ever could.

HAVE WE LEARNED ANYTHING YET? | 39

	Evolution of Symbolism Text			
	Egyptyian Glyphs	Oracle Bones	Mayan Glyphs	Modern Global Icons
Human/ Person				
Sun				
Town/ Village/ City				
Numeral One				

Evolution of written communication throughout history.

DO BETTER. THINK BEYOND SELF.

What I found most interesting when studying history is that many of the values and core beliefs that govern our ancient world are still very much present in modern society. This tells me that the needs and desires of mankind have not changed. Family, survival, power, lust, and wealth rule the humans of this world. All these things are good at the moment, but as history shows, these things are washed away with the days. Why do we desire temporary things?

Say you get all the money you ever can need in the world. You did not have to work another day in your life. No matter how much money you spent, you always had enough money left over. And your neighbor got all the money he needed in the world, and their neighbor got all the money she would ever need. This goes on to everyone from the least to the greatest until everyone in the world has all the money they ever need. What then do we do when everyone can afford anything and everything? How long will the temporary material things (clothes, cars, jewelry, sex, work titles, money) suffice you? What would you then value? What would you live for?

I ask this because this has long been what humanity has built its life on as a means to measure success. If you could have the fastest car, the shiniest jewels, all the men and women you could want to have sex with, and all the money and stuff you could ever buy, would you then be satisfied?

I dare to say that you would not be satisfied. Life living for the temporary is in vain for it is meaningless. I would argue that most will find that once they have all the money they could ever dream to have, they would want to use it to do good in the world. By nature, man wants to improve and bring new life to an area.

There are many stories of people like the "rich and famous" that appear to have it all. The riches, the women, the men, the accolades, the respect, and yet they commit suicide or have serious drug addictions.

What were they missing? What did they discover?

I believe they discovered material possessions do not equate to happiness. Real meaningful relationships with people are what lead to happiness. The rich and famous, royalty, or celebrities still have to get out of bed, feed themselves, wait in traffic, deal with disgruntled people, receive criticism, handle rejection, experience love, and try to maintain their health.

Wealthy people living will tell you that having money does not solve all your problems. Yes, they live life more luxuriously and have the ability to control their lives more efficiently, but they still have to deal with the world the same as me and you. It was not the money that brought them joy, it was the freedom that came with it.

We all have gifts, talents, traits, and characteristics about ourselves that when activated or exercised, can calm a room, repair a relationship, encourage a friend, and invoke change. Those gifts can be used collectively to push humanity to an ultimate goal that is bigger than petty disputes or social injustice. Understand that we are better together, you're needed, and he is needed, and she is needed.

The average person does not want to do destructive acts. They do them based on fear and lack of some sort. I dare you to ask anyone in jail or anyone who has ever committed a crime if they initially wanted to do the activity that led them into that lifestyle. Ask did they dream of becoming a thief when they were a kid. Did they one day hope of becoming a murderer when they were young? What led them to steal, destroy, or kill?

I believe that failure to meet the basic needs of mankind causes cataclysmic stress to the survival of all mankind.

HAVE WE LEARNED ANYTHING YET?

What priority do we put on the material things of our lives? What makes life worth living? Can talent be the currency of life instead of paper bills and metal coins? Is the ultimate goal of life to accumulate wealth and have children? Does blood qualify a person to lead? What should the measure of success look like? Can we learn to treat people fairly based on their qualities that cannot be seen with the eye, but felt through interaction? Can prejudice towards skin color ever be laid to rest?

3

War: What is it Good For?

WAR!... Huuh! GOOD GOD Y'ALL! What is it good for...?

Edwin Starr was on to something with his 1970s smash hit War (What is it Good For)[16]. What is war good for? That's more than a catchy song, it's a legitimate question that should be examined.

Does war solve global or national problems? Is war necessary? Is war a natural part of human existence on this planet? Can peace ever last? What are the effects of past wars? What happens to the loser? Who decides who the enemy is? What good came out of wars of the past? Can we predict the next Global War?

The preceding questions and more will be examined in this chapter.

ORIGINS OF WAR

"History is a bath of blood," wrote William James in his 1906 antiwar essay[17]. "Modern man inherits all the innate pugnacity and all the love of glory of his ancestors. Showing war's irrationality and horror is of no effect on him. The horrors make the fascination. War is the strong life; it is life in extremis; war taxes are the only ones men never hesitate to pay, as the budgets of all nations show us."

The War at Jebel Sahaba (circa~13,000 years ago) is one of the earliest known acts of human armed conflict. Scientists presume that the two tribes that were opposing each other began feuding due to a depletion of natural resources. Presumably, a drought caused waterways to dry up and animals to migrate to the Nile River[18]. The two tribes now found themselves sharing an already shrinking resource. Organized combat may have seemed the easiest way to rid the land of the other tribe and secure the preservation of their own people.

It can be learned from this battle that when a tribe has more to protect, it will defend it at all costs, even if that means killing for it. Brian Ferguson from Scientific American stated in an article, "People fight and kill for personal reasons, but homicide is not war. War is social, with groups organized to kill people from other groups.[19]"

Is that true? Is the act of war business and not personal? Can coexistence prevail over domination?

The word 'war' originates from the Old High German language word, werran meaning to confuse or to cause confusion [20]. Merriam-Webster[21] defines war as a state of usually open and declared hostile armed conflict between states or nations.

So by definition and origin, war is open and declared hostile armed conflict between states or nations that leads to confusion. The mission of war is to confuse and conflict. It succeeds every time.

War shows the ugliest part of mankind. At the root of all wars is the need to protect one's nation or retrieve another nation's possessions at all costs. Leaders persuade their citizens that they are fighting for freedom and their way of life. Citizens are urged to be patriots and help their nation in any way, for the enemy is at hand! Brave citizens courageously volunteer, rally, and buck up! Brave countrymen and women leave their homes, fight, kill, and hopefully conquer to enjoy the freedom and the spoils of war. However, in the aftermath, lives are destroyed, economies collapse, people are displaced from their homes, and lives will never be the same. When the brave soldiers return, if they return, they are horrified by what they saw but also more horrified by what they have done.

If you were to examine the most notorious wars throughout history, you might notice some common characteristics:

- There is a winner and a loser
- Some societal advances occur, while some also detract
- Thousands if not millions of lives are lost
- The countries and their citizens go into crippling debt
- The family structure changes
- Psychological damage lingers in soldiers and families

HAVE WE LEARNED ANYTHING YET?

If we know the devastating and lasting effects of mass conflicts known as war, why do we still use it as a method of persuasion? Have humans evolved to become numb to killing people of other groups? Does war truly protect our freedom? Should the masses have a say in whether a nation should go to war, provided they know all the facts? Just because you can win a fight, does that justify entering a fight? Is war avoidable?

Major Butler said a mouthful in his speech, "War is a racket". In his speech, he said, "War is just a racket. A racket is best described… as something that is not what it seems to the majority of people. Only a small inside group knows what it is about. It is conducted for the benefit of the very few at the expense of the masses." His words and first-hand experience of thirty-three years in active military service made me wonder, could what he said to be true? Behind each war, is there some hidden business agenda that is also being pushed?

When business and national security mix, can the lines become blurred as to why we are fighting a particular enemy? In a similar occurrence, many people believe the war in Iraq in 2001 was really a war over oil. Before the 2003 invasion, Iraq's domestic oil industry was fully nationalized and closed to Western oil companies. President George W. Bush told the American people that the U.S. went to Iraq to retrieve and destroy weapons of mass destruction. After a decade of fighting, no weapon of mass destruction was ever found.

However, a decade of war later, *CNN* reported that the West's largest oil companies have set up shop in Iraq and are reaping an enormous profit. Companies such as ExxonMobil, Chevron, BP, and Shell enjoy the benefits of the 2003 invasion. In addition to a slew of American oil service companies, including Halliburton, the Texas-based firm Dick Cheney ran before becoming George W. Bush's running mate in 2000[23].

War Is Racket

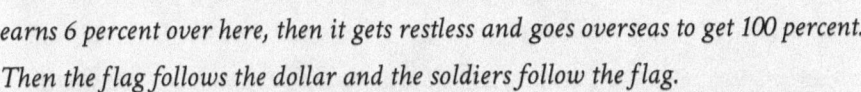

"War is just a racket. A racket is best described, I believe, as something that is not what it seems to the majority of people. Only a small inside group knows what it is about. It is conducted for the benefit of the very few at the expense of the masses.

I believe in adequate defense at the coastline and nothing else. If a nation comes over here to fight, then we'll fight. The trouble with America is that when the dollar only earns 6 percent over here, then it gets restless and goes overseas to get 100 percent. Then the flag follows the dollar and the soldiers follow the flag.

I wouldn't go to war again as I have done to protect some lousy investment of the bankers. There are only two things we should fight for. One is the defense of our homes and the other is the Bill of Rights. War for any other reason is simply a racket.

There isn't a trick in the racketeering bag that the military gang is blind to. It has its "finger men" to point out enemies, its "muscle men" to destroy enemies, its "brain men" to plan war preparations, and a "Big Boss" Super-Nationalistic-Capitalism.

It may seem odd for me, a military man to adopt such a comparison. Truthfulness compels me to. I spent thirty-three years and four months in active military service as a member of this country's most agile military force, the Marine Corps. I served in all commissioned ranks from Second Lieutenant to Major-General. And during that period, I spent most of my time being a high class muscle-man for Big Business, for Wall Street and for the Bankers. In short, I was a racketeer,

> *a gangster for capitalism.*
>
> *I suspected I was just part of a racket at the time. Now I am sure of it. Like all the members of the military profession, I never had a thought of my own until I left the service. My mental faculties remained in suspended animation while I obeyed the orders of higher-ups. This is typical with everyone in the military service.*
>
> *I helped make Mexico, especially Tampico, safe for American oil interests in 1914. I helped make Haiti and Cuba a decent place for the National City Bank boys to collect revenues in. I helped in the raping of half a dozen Central American republics for the benefits of Wall Street. The record of racketeering is long. I helped purify Nicaragua for the international banking house of Brown Brothers in 1909-1912. I brought light to the Dominican Republic for American sugar interests in 1916. In China I helped to see to it that Standard Oil went it's way unmolested.*
>
> *During those years, I had, as the boys in the back room would say, a swell racket. Looking back on it, I feel that I could have given Al Capone a few hints. The best he could do was to operate his racket in three districts. I operated on three continents."*
>
> ~Major General Smedley Butler, USMC
> Excerpt from a speech delivered in 1933, by Major General Smedley Butler, USMC, one of the most decorated marines of all-time[22].

THE SPOILS OF WAR

Historically, war has a unique way of transforming a society and shaping culture. Take, for example, the Persian Wars (492–449 BC) fought between Persia and Greece for almost half a century. The war raged on for about fifty years but eventually yielded to the victory of Greece. For

Greece, the victory not only guaranteed her freedom from foreign rule but also permitted, soon after, an astonishingly rich period of artistic and cultural endeavor which would lay the cultural foundations of all future Western civilizations. It can be assumed had Greece been defeated, the Western world may not have inherited their lasting cultural contributions such as democracy, classical architecture, sculptures, theatre, and the Olympic Games[24].

In the aftermath of the Persian Wars, Greece flourished and entered an age of cultural enrichment that has had a lasting influence even to this day. *So, in this case, was war necessary? If Greece was defeated, would the Western World be what it is today, knowing that many government models are descendants of Ancient Greek democracy? If Persia had won, what type of world would we live in today?*

In most conflicts, one side is mutually agreed to be the winner, and the other is mutually agreed to be the loser. There are also other times when nothing is resolved and the two sides agree to disagree.

In the aftermath of war, the winner typically claims rulership of all or parts of the loser's land, citizens, and economy. The loser can be subject to renaming their country, relinquishing civilian rights and customs, paying imposing taxes, and rebuilding their nation and families. The winner typically maintains their military presence in the now conquered land to monitor and enforce policies. As a humanitarian effort, the winner may help rebuild the losing nation. Often the conquered land will take on the conqueror's characteristics, customs, religion, and language. The idea is for the kingdom's subjects to mirror the ways of the ruling nation.

Treaties also are formed and new alliances are made to prevent future bloodshed and smoother negotiations. In the aftermath, new alliances are also formed in hopes of diplomacy instead of battle. Of wars of the ancient past, the Delian League is one of the first of these alliances formed after the war. The Delian League was established in 478 BC between Greek city-states to be a military alliance to ward off any future Persian attacks[25]. The League, at its greatest size, was composed of over 300 members who paid tribute to Athens, the strongest naval power in Greece; in exchange, Athens would protect its allies with its massive naval fleet. The influence of the Greeks can be seen today in the formation of the United Nations (U.N.).

In the ensuing years after WWII, international leaders proposed creating a new global organization to maintain peace and avoid the abuses of war. The U.N. initially had just fifty-one member states; in 2022, the organization has 193 members. The United Nations has one central mission: the maintenance of international peace and security. The U.N. believes they accomplish this by working to prevent conflict, helping parties in conflict make peace, deploying peacekeepers, and creating the conditions to allow peace to hold and flourish[26]. Major U.N. initiatives include preventing conflict by exploring options to ensure peace, providing food and medical assistance in emergencies, and offering humanitarian support to millions of people around the world. The United Nations has accomplished hundreds of successful peacekeeping missions.

From a historical perspective, war has given some nations a lot of societal advances and freedom. Studies have concluded that since the formation of the United Nations, smaller conflicts have been deterred from turning into major global conflicts. In Ian Morris' book, *War! What is it good for?* [27], Morris argues war is essential to history. He states that only through warfare has humanity been able to come together in larger societies and thus enjoy security and riches. Morris believes it is largely thanks to the past wars that our modern lives are twenty times safer than those of our stone-age ancestors.

Morris states that there has been a 90% decline in the number of violent deaths from war over the past 10,000 years. This is largely attributed to the law and order that comes in reconstructing a society post-war. When the smoke clears and the treaties are signed, the losing or weaker nations are typically overtaken and absorbed into the winning nation. The need for the ruler to maintain order and peace naturally causes an increase in military forces. Morris claims that this need or pressure for safety has a direct correlation to society becoming safer over some time.

HAVE WE LEARNED ANYTHING YET?

I understand Morris' argument and can see the benefits of the social and political changes that occurred in the wake of war, but it still makes me wonder if there is a better way to move humanity forward. Instead of super-powered nations fighting every hundred or so years, could a global focus be reached to promote progress and peace for all of humanity? Because of the numerous wars our ancestors fought, are we now in a place where war is no longer necessary?

THE LOSERS CORNER

It is like a bee and honey, a frog in a pond, an eagle in the sky;

Death and war follow the same rhyme.

One cannot be without the other, for there is no them without the other.

Death and War follow each other like an inseparable sister and brother.

With war, lives will inevitably be lost. As leaders, this is the double-edged sword handed to them when a declaration of war is expressed. There have been over 150 documented wars and conflicts since the early

1200 BC[28]. The total death toll from these wars and conflicts is in the billions. The bloodiest wars depict the dark nature of mankind. In most cases, people will kill for pride and country to defend the actions of a few men and women.

What dispute could be so terrible that it is worth taking the lives of a hundred, thousand, or millions of people? Can we not be civil?

The top five bloodiest wars of all time are World War I, the Taiping Rebellion, the Qing-Ming Conquest, the Mongol Conquest, and World War II. Over 172 million people died in those wars and conquests combined (see Figure 2). That is roughly more than the entire 2022 population of Bangladesh[29], the eighth-most populous country in the world.

The war with the highest death toll was World War II. In 1950 the World Population was around 2.5 billion people. The amount of lives lost in WWII is estimated to be about 70 million. The number of lives lost during World War II alone accounts for about 3% of the entire world's population at that time. Imagine seeing three out of ten men, women, or child worldwide die in war-related activities.

World War II proved to be the deadliest international conflict in history; civilians made up an estimated 50-55 million deaths from the war, while the military comprised 21-25 million lives lost during the war. Millions more were injured, and still more lost their homes and property. War does not solely impact military personnel. War impacts civilian life as well.

Figure 2

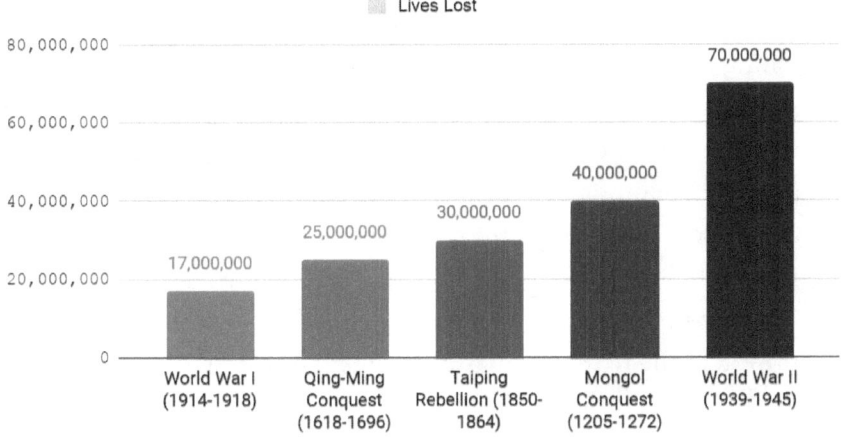

Top 5 Bloodiest Wars of All Time

Civilian populations often have to deal with the effects of war abroad and on the homefront. These conflicts usually damage the infrastructure of hospitals and medical care, often leading to a shortage of doctors. War also has a dramatic impact on the health of civilian populations.

During the colonization years of North America (1492-1763), European diseases from Spain and Britain killed more of the native North American tribes than the sword did. Biological warfare was used during the Seven Years' War (1756–1763). According to the entry in a Captain's ledger, "to convey the smallpox to the Indians" British militia took blankets from their smallpox hospital and gave them as gifts to two neutral Lenape Indian dignitaries during a peace settlement negotiation.[30]

The first global war also helped to spread one of the world's deadliest global pandemics, the Spanish flu epidemic of 1918, which killed an estimated 20 to 50 million people[31]. The instability created in Europe by the First World War (1914-1918) set the stage for another international conflict–World War II–which broke out two decades later and would prove even more devastating.

The hydrogen bombs dropped on the Japanese cities of Hiroshima and Nagasaki in 1945 show the horrendous and long-standing impact of war. Killing thousands was only the beginning. The people in Hiroshima and Nagasaki suffered long-term effects on the population. Children born in those towns contracted radiation sickness and had birth defects long after the buildings destroyed by the bomb were rebuilt[32].

E.O. Wilson said, "We find ourselves in the "battle" to stem an oil spill, the "fight" to tame inflation, the "war" against drugs. Wherever there is an enemy, animate or inanimate, there must be a victory. You must prevail at the front, no matter how high the cost at home.[17]"

HAVE WE LEARNED ANYTHING YET?

How long does it take to see that the battle we are fighting is not one worth winning? Does winning a war change the loser's attitude towards the winner? Should the winner of a war be happy with their victory or should they be ashamed of what they have done? What makes a life decrease in value? What is the value of life unrelated to your family?

THE CASE OF VIETNAM

The Vietnam War (1955-1975)[33] was a long, costly, and divisive conflict that pitted the communist government of North Vietnam against South Vietnam and its principal ally, the United States. In both the United States and Vietnam, the effects of the Vietnam War would linger long after the last American troops returned home in 1973.

The U.S. spent more than $120 billion on the conflict in Vietnam from 1965-1973; this massive spending led to widespread inflation, exacerbated by a worldwide oil crisis in 1973 and skyrocketing fuel prices. Psychologically, the effects ran even deeper.

As the first U.S. troops were withdrawn, those who remained became increasingly angry and frustrated, further escalating problems with morale and leadership. Tens of thousands of soldiers received dishonorable discharges for desertion, and about 500,000 American men from 1965-1973 became "draft dodgers," with many fleeing to Canada to evade going to war.

In Vietnam, more than two decades of violent conflict had inflicted a devastating toll on their population: After years of warfare, an estimated two million Vietnamese were killed and another twelve million became refugees. Warfare demolished the country's infrastructure and economy, and reconstruction proceeded slowly.

The U.S., South Vietnamese forces, North Vietnamese Army, and the Vietcong insurgency deployed millions of land mines. In 2022, there are up to three million pieces of unexploded ordnance and cluster munitions still buried in Vietnam's soil. Clearing the entire country could take up to 100 years and cost billions of dollars, according to officials.

WHAT ABOUT THE CHILDREN?

With the immense number of lives lost during wartime, the families closest to soldiers endure the biggest impact of war, and these effects can drastically alter the family structures. Civilians, especially children, suffer from the effects of war trauma. In an essay written by Joanna Santa Barbara titled, "Impact of War on Children and Imperative to End War"[34] she lists the common impacts of children in war:

> "The impacts in childhood may adversely affect the life trajectory of children far more than adults. Consider children who lose the opportunity for education during war, children who are forced to move into refugee or displaced person camps, where they wait for years in miserable circumstances for normal life to resume, if it ever does. Consider a child disabled in war; they may, in addition to losing a limb, sight, or cognitive capacity, lose the opportunity of schooling and social life. A girl who is raped may be marginalized by her society and lose the opportunity for marriage. Long after the war has ended, these lives will never attain the potential they had before the impact of war."

In the aftermath of World War II, German and Jewish children were often left without parents to help them bear the consequences of war. A group known as The "wolf children" of WWII were forced out of Germany after the war ended. The children wandered hungry through miles of forage, back roads, village towns, and vast forests in order to survive. The journey from East Prussia to Lithuania spans about 280 km or 175 miles by foot. The total number of wolf children has only been estimated. Some say there were up to 25,000 children who roamed the woods and swamps of East Prussia and Lithuania after 1945.

These children were told to go to Lithuania, where there would be food and shelter. Thousands of "Vokietukai," or little Germans in

Lithuanian, passed through villages on their march to the Baltic states. Some locals would leave buckets of soup on their front doors, and others would loose their dogs on the children.

An article written by Volker Wagener of Deutsche Welle, titled "German wolf children: the forgotten orphans of WWII"[35] detailed that young children were more likely to be taken in by families than older children. Boys and girls who didn't find a home had to survive in the woods. Those who got a roof over their heads never knew how long they'd be allowed to stay. Family memories that the orphans had managed to carry with them when they fled — photos, letters, relatives' addresses — were taken from them by their "new parents" and destroyed. Loss of identity was the price of survival.

While the life of the "Vokietukai" was rough in Lithuania, it was still better than the fate that awaited those who were too weak to make it to the Baltic states. Thousands of these children were sent to Soviet homes run by the military administration. That was the fate of some 4,700 German children in 1947, according to historian Ruth Leiserowitz, who has researched the fates of wolf children[36].

Many of them were sent later that year to the Soviet occupation zone, which later became the German Democratic Republic (GDR). They traveled in freight trains without anything to sleep on. The children, who ranged from two to sixteen years of age, arrived in East Germany after four days and four nights; exhausted, famished, and parentless. Upon arrival, they were put in orphanages or adopted by avid Communists.

* * *

Imagine being told that your whole city has 48 hours to evacuate and leave all that you have behind. Take what you can carry and travel 200 miles west. Assuming you and your family are walking, what's going through your mind? What if you were eleven years old and alone? The battlefield is no place for children, but modern warfare has brought the battle straight to their homes.

In recent years the fighting in the region of Sudan has been notorious for forcing children to join their army. It is estimated that tens of thousands of young people under eighteen serve in militias in about sixty countries[37]. The children range in age from 6-18 and beyond that, you are typically killed. Some children are even forced to murder their own parents in order to survive. To this day, young girls are being kidnapped in the hundreds from their schools in broad daylight with nobody able to stop the bandits.

These innocent lives are forced to grow up within a matter of days to weeks and fight for their own survival. Unfortunately, when most of these children grow up to become adults, they will have a tarnished mentality and have difficulty having meaningful relationships. These children will eventually shape a future that was neglectful to them in their past.

A child is one victim of war, but what about the soldiers? What's the significance of a few good men and women dying if by their deaths they save their country? How can soldiers assimilate back into society after everything they saw and did on the battlefield? Is a soldier considered a victim if they understand the magnitude of active military service?

As a soldier, the dangers are real, the possibility of war is always and life is a constant set of orders. Sympathy for the pawns in war is short-lived as the decisions of a few keep the battle raging on for the many.

As a soldier involved in active military combat, there is an inner struggle between not wanting to kill, but also doing your duty as a soldier and having to kill. Your military contract dictates that you agree to follow orders and protect your nation with your life. If called to combat, you must kill the enemy or risk being killed yourself, or worst risk the lives of everyone in your platoon. To follow orders is to commit murder, but to not follow orders is to commit treason. Many soldiers are ashamed of what they have done when they come back from combat. In addition, they have a limited number of people from home with whom they can share their experiences with.

Would a mother understand the things that her baby boy did in the line of duty? Would a hometown friend be able to relate to the sensation you feel seeing your enemy come into your rifle's crosshairs? Did that "enemy" truly deserve to die or was he only also following orders to defend his home? One thing is certain the person that left home for military combat is not the same person returning home afterward.

According to *history.com* The later years of the Vietnam War saw increased physical and psychological deterioration among American soldiers, including drug use, post-traumatic stress disorder, mutinies, and attacks by soldiers against officers and noncommissioned officers. On the homefront, many returning veterans from Vietnam faced negative reactions from opponents of the war (who viewed them as having killed innocent civilians) and its supporters (who saw them as having lost the war)[33]. This type of physical and psychological deterioration is seen in the lives of most soldiers, past and present.

There is an upside to being a soldier. The community within military life encourages soldiers to support one another. It is a brotherhood unlike anything else most people will experience. Soldiers gain lifelong friends, get to travel the world, and have many of their basic needs met. A soldier learns a level of discipline most people will never experience, in addition to monetary incentives and benefits such as covered tuition, healthcare, and retirement savings. A soldier's life is complicated and filled with uncertainty. Civilians may never understand the full magnitude of gratitude due to the soldiers fighting for their nation.

HAVE WE LEARNED ANYTHING YET?

Are the physical and psychological effects of war worth the battle? Is a person's quality of life protected in war or dismantled? Will the territory conquered truly help a nation live better? What will we have to give up to gain something new? At what point do we choose to value life over death and destruction? What provokes us to want to slaughter thousands of people?

WAS GOOD ESTABLISHED?

I would be remiss if I did not mention that some good social and cultural changes have come out of war. The alliances that form after wartime have brought generational peace to certain parts of the world. The Delian League required members to submit a monetary tax payable to Athens for protection. Athens could continue to maintain and improve its massive navy and league members could find protection for less than it would cost to maintain autonomous forces[46]. The Delian League fostered the way for future alliances such as the United Nations, which has mediated numerous peacekeeping missions to prevent conflict and use diplomacy rather than violence.

Wartime efforts often call for weapon manufacturers to make stronger and more powerful weapons. The existence of these stronger and more powerful weapons can often serve as a deterrent for future battles. The inventions of nuclear warheads in World War II have fostered nuclear deterrence and international agreements to reduce the likelihood of global conflict resulting in the usage of nuclear weapons[38]. Nuclear weapons that if activated and launched, would kill hundreds of millions of lives. Since the invention of nuclear weapons around 1945, there has not been another global war of the same magnitude as WWII.

> *"To fight and conquer in all your battles is not supreme excellence; supreme excellence consists in breaking the enemy's resistance without fighting... Therefore the skillful leader subdues the enemy's troops without any fighting... With his forces intact he will dispute the mastery of the Empire, and thus, without losing a man, his triumph will be complete."*
> -Sun Tzu *(Chinese founder of strategic military thinking)*

Sometimes a successful defense in war can also establish an assumed weaker country's position and set them on the path of independence for centuries. Burma's successful defense in the Sino-Burmese War (1765-1769) laid the foundation for the present-day boundary between China and Burma (Myanmar).[39]

War can also be beneficial in spreading a nation's ideals, beliefs, and traditions to a wider population. Rome's military dominance and Rome's legal institution were vital in the empire's ability to spread its culture and beliefs to many nations. Their influence has reached a time beyond its own empire and nations that were never under Roman rule.

World War I brought about massive social upheaval, as millions of women entered the workforce to support men who went to war and replace those who never returned. With millions of men away from home, women filled manufacturing and agricultural positions on the home front. Others provided support on the front lines as nurses, doctors, ambulance drivers, translators, and, in rare cases, on the battlefield. Black American women were able to make their first major shift from domestic employment to work in offices and factories.

Some nations have found ways to cope with the aftermath of war through reparations to the families most impacted, monuments built of war heroes, and new leadership to bring the people into a new era.

As the days move forward, people by nature also move forward. There is no stopping time. Those who watched the war from the comfort of tv screens or heard about it in letters quickly return to business as usual.

But for those closely impacted, the soldiers, or the dismantled family, may get some comfort from small support groups for a short while. But eventually, they too will be expected to move on and assimilate back to civilian life on the home front. I imagine therapy helps a little, but once alone, the battle in the mind resumes. This is the most difficult and longest battle a person will ever have to fight.

Will we ever reach a period when we deem war no longer necessary? Or will an enemy always arise that would need to be defeated?

CAN WAR BE ELIMINATED?

Throughout this chapter, we have learned how wars are started, the wreckage that occurs during wartime, and the aftermath of war. Many wars have been started by one nation or one leader's desire to possess more than what they currently have. People who want more than their lot in life. A nation's desire for more land, a nation's desire for more control over oil, a nation's desire to spread their religion, and a nation's desire to eliminate a certain group of people have been at the root of most wars throughout history—the desire to want or covet someone else's possessions.

If we go back to divine law, as discussed in Chapter 2, we can understand why it was written to not covet your neighbor's possessions in the Ten Commandments. When you desire someone else's possessions, you will do just about anything to get them. This leads to poor decision-making and, in some cases, the loss of life. The same law can be applied to political decision-making. If a decision to invade someone's land is based on the desire to have what that nation has, that decision should not be acted on.

Be satisfied with what your nation is producing and, if necessary, peaceably trade with other nations to share resources. This land we live on is a gift to each person. No one person created oil, trees, gold, diamonds, sugar, cotton, or any other raw material. All were gifted to us by the Creator. Our ancestors set up shop in an area and claimed it as their own. Today we are fighting over lands that our ancestors discovered. If we are to do better as mankind, we must first understand that this world was gifted to us to tend to the land, reproduce its fruits, and innovate new objects and systems.

We can do all these things if we focus collectively as one- together. Forget the petty disputes that lead to death. Forget the hasty declarations that lead to poverty. Forget the covetous desires that lead to strife. We can be better than our ancestors if we decide to refocus our efforts and not desire what does not belong to us in the first place and share in the riches of this world.

4

History Repeats Itself

For everything, there is a season,
A time for every activity under heaven. A time to be born and a time to die.
A time to plant and a time to harvest. A time to kill and a time to heal.
A time to tear down and a time to build up.
A time to cry and a time to laugh.
A time to grieve and a time to dance.
A time to scatter stones and a time to gather stones.
A time to embrace and a time to turn away.
A time to search and a time to quit searching.
A time to keep and a time to throw away.
A time to tear and a time to mend.
A time to be quiet and a time to speak.
A time to love and a time to hate.
A time for war and a time for peace.

~ Ecclesiastes 3:1-8 Amplified Bible

There is a time for everything in life. History shows we ebb and flow through seasons of happiness, sadness, uncertainty, and clarity. These life cycles are not singular to one generation or geographic region but are echoed throughout the world in every generation. Certain stories or aspects of life seem to repeat generation after generation. Human nature is the one element of life that has not evolved since the beginning of creation.

The same desires, needs, and characteristics of people, such as love, family, and duty, have existed since the beginning of our existence. Because of this, we can relate to our ancestors' struggles and triumphs even though we lived in different time periods. As humans evolved, we needed a way to pass down beliefs and culture. Humans learned that these lessons are easier to pass down if written. In the Mesopotamian era, scribes documented laws, war stories, medicines, recipes, maps, and religious doctrine. Some stories were meant to glorify the protagonist, while others were meant to instill virtues to improve the next generation. Many of their stories are situations we can relate to today in modern society.

Take, for example, the first recorded customer complaint nearly 4,000 years ago. As the story goes, a man named Nanni expressed his extreme displeasure to the merchant Ea-Nasir about a recent copper shipment. Nanni's story was written on a clay tablet in cuneiform and found thousands of years later by archaeologists.

The following is the translated complaint:
"When you came, you said to me as follows,
'I will give Gimil-Sin (when he comes) fine quality copper ingots.'
You left then, but you did not do what you promised me. You put ingots that were not good before my messenger and said, 'If you want to take them, take them; if you do not want to take them, go away!'
What do you take me for, that you treat somebody like me with such contempt...Take cognizance that (from now on) I will not accept

here any copper from you that is not of fine quality. I shall (from now on) select and take the ingots individually in my own yard, and I shall exercise against you my right of rejection because you have treated me with contempt."[44]

It seems moral law is in effect here. People deserve and expect to be treated fairly; wrongful actions will cause distrust and strife. I also learned that there have always been shady business owners! And to think that you are not the first person to have ever been cheated out of your money. Moreover, this behavior, attitude, or respect is not new to the 21st Century. Respect has always been a virtue that is valued, commanded and at times demanded by peers and subordinates.

The poor service that Nanni's messenger received is not unlike a situation that could occur today between a disgruntled customer and a stubborn business owner. When you strip away the fancy gadgets, clothes, and languages, it's easy to see people as people and parts of human nature have not changed in many centuries. The core beliefs, values, and sense of what is proper and in good measure are innate laws that have lingered with us for centuries.

One story that might be familiar to most is the story of *Cain and Abel*[2]. The story of *Cain and Abel* is acknowledged as one of the first murders in the history of mankind. According to ancient texts, Cain and Abel were the first sons of Adam and Eve, who were the first humans ever created.

Cain was the eldest son and Abel was the younger brother. As the story goes, Abel kept flocks, and Cain worked the soil. One day, Cain prepared an offering to the Lord using some fruits from his field. Abel also brought an offering of fat portions from some of the firstborn animals in his flock. The Lord respected Abel and his offering, but he did not look favorably on Cain and his offering. Cain became angry and jealous of his brother. His anger rose to the point that he asked his brother to come to the field with him one day. When he thought nobody was looking, Cain attacked and killed his brother Abel. After it was known what Cain had done to his brother, he was exiled from his father's land and was cursed with struggling to grow anything from his crops as long as he lived.

HAVE WE LEARNED ANYTHING YET?

This story has been passed down over many generations to teach people the cost of jealousy, anger, and murder. The story of Cain and Abel shows up in the Torah, the Old Testament, and The Quran. Their story can serve as a deterrent for murder and jealousy. If the first sons of humanity struggled with jealousy, why have we humans today not evolved past this archaic emotion? Why do people still commit murder if we have seen in past times the result? Why do we repeat behavior that leads to an undesirable end?

Aesop was a famous Greek storyteller around 500 BC that helped spread virtue through storytelling. In his story *The Bundle of Sticks*[45] he parables the importance of unity:

A certain Father had a family of sons who were forever quarreling among themselves. No words he could say did the least good, so he cast about in his mind for some very striking example that should make them see that discord would lead them to misfortune.

One day when the quarreling had been much more violent than usual and each of the sons was moping in a surly manner, he asked one of them to bring him a bundle of sticks. Then handing the bundle to each of his sons, in turn, he told them to try to break it. But although each one tried his best, none was able to do so.

The Father then untied the bundle and gave the sticks to his sons to break one by one. This they did very easily.

"My sons," said the Father, "do you not see how certain it is that if you agree with each other and help each other, it will be impossible for your enemies to injure you? But if you are divided among yourselves, you will be no stronger than a single stick in that bundle."

In unity is strength.

This story teaches the importance of unity, togetherness, and the results of division. This story has been used in many publications throughout history and provides a timeless lesson of unity in strength.

There are countless other stories like *Cain and Abel* or *The Bundle of Sticks* that show the error in human emotion or thinking and provide a way to be better. Mankind has had over 200,000 years to learn from these stories and make changes. Why haven't we? Why are we still making the same mistakes as our ancient ancestors?

HAVE WE LEARNED ANYTHING YET?

Are our emotions a blessing or a curse? Can we evolve from our insufficient primordial emotions such as jealousy, hatred, and envy? Does unity in strength only pertain to small kinships, groups, or nations? Can unity in strength pertain to all of humanity? Is it possible to unite mankind to be stronger together and move us beyond the minor squabbles that divide us? If history is repeated by each generation fighting the same moral battles, what hope do we have in improving the world?

* * *

What profit is there for the worker from that in which he labors? I have seen the task which God has given to the sons of men with which to occupy themselves. He has made everything beautiful and appropriate in its time.

He has also planted eternity [a sense of divine purpose] in the human heart [a mysterious longing which nothing under the sun can satisfy, except God]—yet man cannot find out (comprehend, grasp) what God has done (His overall plan) from the beginning to the end.

I know that there is nothing better for them than to rejoice and to do good as long as they live; and also that every man should eat and drink and see and enjoy the good of all his labor—it is the gift of God.

I know that whatever God does, it endures forever; nothing can be added to it nor can anything be taken from it, for God does it so that men will fear and worship Him [with awe-filled reverence, knowing that He is God]. That which has already been, and that which will be has already been, for God seeks what has passed by [so that history repeats itself].

Ecclesiastes 3:9-15 Amplified Bible

In Solomon's Poem (Ecclesiastes 3:9-15 see above), he describes the task that God, The Creator, gives mankind to busy themselves while alive. Solomon eludes in his last sentence that God recalls what has passed so that history will repeat itself. Why would the Creator of the Universe design life to repeat itself?

Imagine solving a Rubik's cube every day for eternity, or watching the same four seasons of your favorite show for the rest of eternity, gaining weight, losing weight for the rest of eternity, fighting and loving for the rest of eternity. Why would anyone want to repeat life's cycle over and over for eternity?

In my understanding, The Creator does not want history to necessarily repeat itself; it's more about the law of the universe. The laws which regulate this world do not change; therefore, the same actions will cause the same reactions; the same reactions will cause the same actions. The same problems will always produce the same results. The universe will bring back to view, recall again into being that which was past and had vanished out of sight and out of mind.

If we humans cannot learn from our mistakes, we are doomed to repeat them. The dates may change, the buildings will improve, and the technology can be far advanced, but the laws that govern this world will remain.

So what am I saying? Be a goodie-goodie your whole life? Or be robotic with no emotion so we don't repeat history?

- Precisely Not.

Moreover, understand the nature of the world and the people that live in it. In pursuit of creating a society or environment that complements human nature's strengths and weaknesses. A flower needs good soil and water to bloom. If you understand that, you can produce an environment for nature to take its course, allowing the flower to bloom as it should. If you do not understand the flowers' needs and nature, you will neglect them, abuse them, and ultimately kill them.

The purpose of studying history is to make us better, better as individuals, and better as citizens. The study of history has a moral purpose as well. The lessons of history have shown us that human nature has not changed or evolved. All the human emotions are the same today as in Egypt in the days of the Pharaohs or in China in the time of the Dynasties or during the reign of the Roman Empire: love, hate, ambition, kindness, generosity, promiscuity, jealousy, and the lust for power. The good and bad of human nature are simply poured into new vessels.

The American Founders believed when one person controls the entire nation; human selfishness will negatively influence their ability to rule. They attempted to improve how rulers governed their people and formed a democratic nation that votes in its leaders and cycles them on a four-year basis. They also put checks and balances in place so that the executive, judicial, and legislative branches balance each other out and shift power accordingly. This was unlike the Monarchs and Emperors of the past who were born into royalty or took it by force and stayed in power until death. By forging a democratic republic, the United States has been able to change the course of its history and produce a country that is a desired place to live by people all around the world.

ENTERPRISE OVER HUMANITY

Throughout history, there are many examples where enterprise or societal advancements occurred at the expense of oppressing other people. The Egyptian pyramids were built on the backs of Israelite slaves. The British Empire was expanded by overtaking and colonizing Indian and African nations. The Japanese unification of territories was made possible by the deaths of many warriors and Buddhist monks. The United States achieved prosperity through the mass enslavement and forced labor of generations of African people.

Enterprise over humanity has a history of repeating throughout every generation, dynasty, and empire. Enterprise has given way to many architectural wonders, riches, and inventions. But are the monuments, the money, and tools justifiable in the suffering of the oppressed? Do the means always justify the ends?

In American history, students are often taught history from a high-level overview of behaviors and actions from the 1800s till the present. Students are taught that enslaved people were brutally treated and received low to no wages. From my studies, I noticed that there was not much information or focus on the business model of the plantations. Enslavement must have been pretty important to the livelihoods of the eleven southern states of the then United States for southerners to rebel against the White House for wanting to grant freedom to enslaved people.

Slavery's purpose in The Slave Trade was not to punish African people but rather, slavery was a tool to establish the country's infrastructure and bring wealth into the states. The Africans taken from their homelands to America were skilled in growing and harvesting crops.

Slave owners were actually business owners who made enormous profits by exercising free labor.

In 1844, the largest plantation owner in his time was William Aiken Jr; also known as the largest slave owner in American history. Aiken was one of the state's wealthiest citizens, owner of the largest rice plantation in the state, and the 61st Governor of South Carolina. By 1860, Aiken owned the entire Jehossee Island in South Carolina. This property was immaculate and was about 1,500 acres, about the size of 1,100 football fields. Aiken owned over 800 enslaved African and Indians. Like Aiken, many of the planter aristocrats of that time did not have the know-how to bring forth bountiful crops. They relied on the knowledge of their slaves brought from their homeland. Today, descendants of the Aiken family, the Maybanks, still own part of the island.[46]

After the Civil War, Aiken's plantation regained its prominence and the plantation produced 1.5 million pounds of rice in addition to sweet potatoes and corn. During this time, rice was king in South Carolina and was one of the ten largest cash crops. An extremely wealthy planter, Aiken made a fortune producing cotton and rice. His fortune also allowed him to be equally successful in his investments in railroads and other businesses. Outside of shelter, food, and clothing, he shared little of his fortune with the people that were in the fields doing the work. By 1860 census takers valued his real and personal estates at $290,600[47] (estimated 9 million 2020 U.S. Dollars).

Slavery has always been beneficial to everyone but the slaves. To this day, little appreciation is shown to the enslaved people who tilled American soil, which brought in unprecedented wealth for the country. The generational wealth that many White Americans enjoy today was provided to them by the hands of African people.

This is true in ancient times as well; the Israelites profited little from building Egypt until their great deliverance and mass exodus. As the

HAVE WE LEARNED ANYTHING YET? | 73

Israelites left, they plundered Egypt and took with them gold, silver, and clothing.

In many ancient civilizations, the people all worked for the King or Emperor. There were only two classes: Royalty and everyone else. Everyone else built the pyramids, the walls, the royal palaces, the stadiums, the amphitheaters, and the colosseums. Everyone else planted the food and bred the cattle. Royalty made the decrees, gave orders, and provided means to accomplish their vision. Royalty or, in modern times, the elite have always reaped the harvest off everyone else.

Oppression exists today in less obvious forms. Oppression relies heavily on the oppressed person being intimidated either by the threat of violence or by some other method of abuse. Today people willingly offer their services in exchange for money. The job-owner agrees to pay for their services according to their belief of what the person is worth. The oppressed have little say over their worth evaluation. Essentially it's, "Take it or leave it; what one won't do, another will."

This mental psyche and the need for people to provide for their families keeps many people serving for less than they are worth and keeps the power in the hands of the job owner. Physical abuse is rarely seen in the workplace now, but mental abuse is very common. Mental abuse can make you doubt your own feelings and thoughts, and even your sanity, by others manipulating the truth.

There is some hope of a shift in fairness in the common workplace. One CEO by the name of Dan Price, increased his minimum salary for employees to $70,000 USD. According to an article in Inc. Magazine[48], while other companies were cutting employees, he decided to increase the salary of his employees. By making this shift, the company's revenue tripled and more employees were able to purchase homes. This model is proof that fairness over oppression increases loyalty and production.

HAVE WE LEARNED ANYTHING YET?

Is progress possible without oppression? If humans are working towards a common goal, should pay reflect equally? Is enterprise over humanity a sustainable model?

DON'T REPEAT HISTORY

"The most important thing we learned from the past is that we never learn from the past. Time after time, new empires make the same mistakes as old empires, rich and powerful people get corrupted by their power and wealth, militaristic regimes always go one step too far and get destroyed, fiat money not backed by a commodity such as gold always collapses, the 'peasants' are always repressed until they revolt[49]."

-shortbaldman, Reddit

What if the lessons learned from our ancestors were incorrect? Or at least relevant and useful during that time when our grandparents and great grandparents were growing up. Their thoughts, feelings, and ways of life.

As humanity adapts and learns, we often realize that there was some error in what grandpa had previously perceived to be true. Alvin Toffler, an American writer, futurist, and businessman, is credited with saying:

"The illiterate of the 21st century will not be those who cannot read and write, but those who cannot learn, unlearn, and relearn."

Many believe that cold air will give you a cold or illness. Studies have shown that quite the opposite is true.

"No matter what your grandmother might have told you, spending too much time in the cold air does not make you sick." Shannon Fecher, ARNP, from UnityPoint Health stated[50], "Viruses tend to occur more in colder seasons, as we spend a lot of time indoors, which allows the virus to spread more readily. Instead of the cold weather causing illness, it can actually help prevent you from getting sick. It's actually encouraged to go out even in the colder months for exercise and activities, as staying inside among others puts you at higher risk of getting ill."

The US Department of Agriculture tells us that adults should drink three cups of milk daily, mostly for calcium and vitamin D. The "Got Milk?" ad campaign from the 90s promoted drinking milk for strong bones. While small amounts of dairy milk will provide some calcium, too much could lead to more serious health conditions. Multiple studies show that there isn't an association between drinking more milk (or taking calcium and vitamin D supplements) and having fewer bone fractures. Some studies have even shown an association with higher overall mortality, prostate cancer, eczema, and acne [51,52].

In another example, take the ever-changing relationship between humans, cannabis, and our health. Most ancient cultures didn't grow the plant to get high, but as herbal medicine, likely starting in Asia around 500 BC. The history of cannabis cultivation in America dates back to the early colonists, who grew hemp for textiles and rope.

The jazz age of the 1920s brought the recreational use of cannabis to mainstream society. During that time, cannabis was widely used in most jazz clubs. Political and racial fears of Black teens and White teens mingling together led to the criminalization of marijuana in the United States and mass incarceration[53].

In the 1940s, a slew of false marketing campaigns was shown to the public in movie theaters, newspapers, and news broadcasts to get people to fear using cannabis led by Harry J. Anslinger (head of the Federal Bureau of Narcotics)[54]. In response to the misinformation campaigns, New York City Mayor Fiorello La Guardia commissioned a blue-ribbon panel of leading doctors, psychiatrists, psychologists, pharmacologists, chemists, and sociologists and tasked them with making a thorough investigation of cannabis based on a comprehensive review of all available scientific literature, plus primary research.

What they found was contrary to everything Anslinger and the team had been promoting about cannabis. Released as The La Guardia Report, the landmark study earned the endorsement of the prestigious New York Academy of Medicine the following is a summary of their findings:

> "Marijuana, like alcohol, does not alter the basic personality," the report's authors concluded. "Marijuana does not of itself give rise to antisocial behavior. There is no evidence to suggest that the continued use of marijuana is a stepping stone to the use of opiates. Prolonged drug use does not lead to physical, mental, or moral degeneration, nor have we observed any permanent deleterious effects from its continued use. On the contrary, marijuana and its derivatives and allied synthetics have potentially valuable therapeutic applications that merit future investigation. [55]"

Since then, there have been numerous studies that advocate for cannabis and its potential health benefits. Every generation in every specialized field needs people with curiosity, like La Guardia researchers. People that are a bit rebellious and do not believe everything that is taught to them. Those types of people help accelerate progress, transform mindsets, challenge preconceived notions, and reject conformity.

This is true for everyday situations for everyday people. **You do not have to be some world-changer to affect change.** Begin with curiosity, and look at a problem with a new eye.

HAVE WE LEARNED ANYTHING YET?

Consider long feuds amongst family. How many years will go by without reconciliation? Can we discover the truth from all sides, consider each other's perspectives, and forgive on a human level?

Do you know why you do what you do? Do you know why you prefer a certain brand of toothpaste? Or why do you trust a certain brand of car? Could it be because your parents bought that brand when you were a kid? Do you know why they trusted that brand?

Are your parents' values, ones that you care about? If so, all is well. If not, you can now **DECIDE** *to make a change.*

Thoughts, ideas, and feelings are allowed and should change with each generation. It is the duty of each new generation to discover its own truth. Discover what is real to them and what is fair and worthwhile in this world. Use what lessons our forefathers have learned, apply the solution, and evaluate the result. If the result is favorable, then what was learned may still be true. If the result is unfavorable, then what is learned may need to be reevaluated to measure accuracy.

Now cannabis smoking and associations with cold air and sickness are not the only examples throughout history where people got it wrong the first time; below are a few others. Can you think of any others that are not listed?:

- **Women have no business in business, politics, or voting:** Prior to the 1920s, women in America were seen as keepers of the house and children. They were not allowed to vote, own property, or hold positions in office. After over 100 years of protesting, women in the U.S. women gained equal rights and the right to vote in 1920. Today women in the U.S. represent over half of the workforce and hold various levels of position in all disciplines, including business, medical, and government.
- **Jewish people are inferior and White Skin and Blue Eyed people are the superior race:** In WWII, Germany's Leader, Adolf Hitler, believed this was true and surprisingly got a majority of Germany to believe the same thing. Today, most people renounce Hitler's platform and everything he represented and do not believe Jewish people are inferior by any means. Jewish citizens have made major strides worldwide in science, business, politics, and the arts.
- **Black people, like children, are incapable of making their own decisions and being societal leaders:** This idea kept White control over Black slaves. It was not that Black people were incapable of complex ideas; it was that Black people were not given the opportunity to be educated. Today this notion has been proven to be preposterous. Even still without formal education, many slaves, including Fredrick Douglas and Harriet Tubman, were self-educated and made lasting contributions to American and Canadian society.
- **Earth is Flat:** The myth of Flat Earth is a modern misconception that the Earth is flat rather than spherical. Many scholars during the Middle Ages in Europe spread this belief. It has since been proved through research and various space missions that, indeed the earth is round.

It is important to continue to learn, unlearn and relearn new concepts and ideas throughout your life. You may find that your fear is not your own, but yet it was something that you were pre-exposed to as a child. Or beliefs you had were based on generations of relatives' thoughts and beliefs.

If you despise a certain race of people, consider why. What about their way of life do you despise? Are you guilty of doing the same things? Is it a race issue or a human issue?

Do you think 1920s, John D. Rockefeller could explain the importance of social media and business in 2022? Or would that conversation be better suited for someone who has relevant experience from this generation, like Mark Zuckerberg? Rockefeller undoubtedly, if he were alive today, could consult businesses on several ways to improve business based on his years of experience. However, he would not be the go-to guy to explain how likes, retweets, hashtags, and viral videos would improve business.

In life, we must choose to accept the truth and reject false beliefs. We must choose carefully who we learn from and what advice we let enter our subconscious. We must not stop learning, educating ourselves, or being curious at the age of eighteen. Everything we have learned up until that age was taught by either an institution, family, or friends. At that age, we have limited experiences of our own that test our learned beliefs.

HAVE WE LEARNED ANYTHING YET?

Have an honest conversation with yourself and explain to yourself why you believe what you believe. If you do not have all the answers, go back to the source that taught you this belief. Is their belief based on sound doctrine or a credible source?

Consider this tale,

A beautiful young woman recently came of age and like all first-born women in her family, when they become eighteen, their mothers passed down the family ring. The ring was simple, a large heart hugging a smaller heart, all covered in silver. Inside the smaller heart was a tiny socket where a stone had once been.

The ladies always talked about adding a new stone to it, but nobody wanted to risk tarnishing the mojo or essence of the ring. The ring was known for its magical charm. Every lady that has worn the ring has found love shortly after receiving the ring and all the women that wore that ring have birthed a daughter first.

A few years later, after the young lady received the family ring, she married a man, and a year after that, she became pregnant with a girl. With her first daughter forming inside her, she found herself elated that she one day would have the privilege of continuing the tradition of the women in her family. With the thought of passing her ring down one day, she became curious about the origin of the ring.

She thought to herself, "Who initially bought the ring? Why was it given? What happened to the stone that is now missing from its setting?"

She went to her mother and asked her what she knew about the ring. Her mother laughed bashfully, embarrassed because she never thought to ask. The only thing she knew was that the ring had been passed down to her from her mother and her mother received it from her mother's mother before that. Thankful for her first clue, the pregnant mother leaves to visit her grandmother.

After enjoying some warm tea and cookies with her grandmother, the young woman asked her grandmother about the ring.

"Grandmother, Can you tell me what you know about our family ring? Who initially bought the ring? Why was it given? What happened to the stone that is now missing from its setting?"

"Ahh..., the family ring." As she says this, grandmother glances briefly into the distance as if remembering a very special memory. Her face began to light up and the pregnant woman could see that this was a very fond memory. "I remember the day my mom gave me that ring; it was beautiful. She had just picked it up from the jeweler who had cleaned and polished the ring and also smooth it back out after years of wear. My mother gave it to me when I was eighteen like your mother did, and like I did for your mother, my mother did for me."

"As for the missing stone, I am not sure. My mother and grandmother worked hard for everything they had, so I did not want to embarrass them by asking."

Now embarrassed herself, the young woman hung her head and her cheeks began to get hot and flushed with color.

Grandmother continues, "But I remember overhearing a conversation with my mom and grandmother about a boy named Kenton. I remember this because this was in my grandmother's old age. She had developed Alzheimer's and frequently confused the past with the present. In one of these moments on the very day of my eighteenth birthday, mom was trying to calm grandmother down. She was hysterical and kept saying the ring was stolen and that Kenton won't be happy when he finds out. Mother gently walked my grandmother to her room and the party went on. Mother claimed grandmother was a bit loony and not to mind her, so I did and that was the last I heard about it. Come to think of it; I haven't thought about that name since then."

"Wow, Grandmother that is some story, do you think this Kenton boy could have bought this ring for my Great-great-grandmother?"

"Not sure, but you can ask my mother if she still has some of her marbles!" Grandmother chuckles hysterically and brews another pot of tea.

The next day, the young woman set out to Riverfront Senior Living Home to visit her 96-year-old great-grandmother. Upon checking in, the young woman finds her great-grandmother sitting grumpily outside her room.

In her prime, great-grandmother was a boss! She held numerous positions in the community and was known for her tough but fair leadership. Even in her old age, her great-grandmother was still tough.

The young lady brewed a cup of coffee and sat across from her great-grandmother. Her great-grandmother had not moved a muscle since she had been there. Not even a slight eye following to acknowledge her presence.

"Great-grandmother, I'm pregnant with my first daughter! I am very excited to one day pass this ring to my daughter and share with my daughter the story behind this ring and its tradition. Can you tell me what you know about the ring? How did it come into our family and why?"

Great-grandmother sat there silent and unmoving. Eyes empty.

Great-grandmother, please, you are my last hope! What do you know about this ring?" The young lady lifted her hand closer to her great-grandmother's face, showing off the ring on her finger. "Who is Kenton!?"

At the name of Kenton, Great-grandmother raised her head.

"Kenton was my high school sweetheart. He gifted me with this ring for my eighteenth birthday and asked for my hand in marriage. I was blown away and obviously excited. I gave myself to him that night and it was a very good night. A few weeks later, Kenton was arrested for robbery. You see, Kenton wanted to marry me but did not have enough money for a proper ring. He did not believe my father would allow me to marry him without it. His buddies stole other things that night, along with my ring, and long story short, Kenton went to jail for eighteen or so years.

Meanwhile, I still have the ring and 2 months later, I found out that I was to be a mother. Scared of the influence an inmate might have on my child, I hid that information from Kenton. I knew the consequences of my actions but made peace with my decision.

Raising her without him wasn't easy, but I believed it would be better that way. I knew she longed for a father, but I was too far in to turn back. I got the idea to pass down the ring to her on her eighteenth birthday as a twisted and silent memento of past and future. I told her the ring came from my mother, but really it came from Kenton."

The young woman sat there in amazement. She was basically just told that her great-grandfather stole the very ring she has on her finger, went to jail for it, and unknowingly impregnated her great-grandmother. This was a lot of information to digest, if you can imagine.

"Where is Kenton now?"

"Not sure, probably dead. I tried staying in contact with him for a few years while he was in prison - not mentioning our daughter, of course- But prison changes a man and life as a single mother changed mine. Eventually, we stopped talking; by the time he was released, we moved to another city and I never saw him again."

***

How would you feel after hearing that story? Put yourself in the young woman's place. The ring your family for generations held sacred was actually stolen by your great-grandfather that nobody knew existed. The magic was gone, the truth a lie to cover up shame.

Now that you know the truth, would you pass the ring down to your next generation or would it stop with you?

This story is similar to generational hatred, generational feuds, and generational lies. Unknown history can cause future generations to live out what is not true. Even if the truth is never revealed, be curious to find the truth and find your own morals. Change can happen in everyday activities. You do not have to be a world leader to affect change. Change first must happen within yourself.

HAVE WE LEARNED ANYTHING YET?

What generational cycles could you be living out that were founded on poor decision-making? How do you honor the past but not be hindered by it? What is the balance of necessary change and radical change?

5

The Law of Truth

"We hold these truths to be self-evident, that all men are created equal, that they are endowed by The Creator with certain unalienable Rights, that among these are Life, Liberty and the pursuit of Happiness."
  -Declaration of Independence (United States of America)

Imagine a gardener pouring gasoline in their garden because they believed that gasoline was what the garden needed to move the roots to good soil faster. Week after week, the gardener pours gasoline on the grass, flowers, shrubs, and trees. The gardener becomes frustrated that the garden is not growing yet dying day by day.

To remedy the problem, the gardener says, "Let me add sugar to the gasoline so that the food will taste sweeter." After weeks of trying this, the gardener became irate with the garden for still not growing. The gardener shouts, "I give you gas to move your roots and sugar to sweeten your fruits, and yet you still do not produce a blade of grass, a flower petal, not even a sprout! To hell with you garden!"

The gardener strikes a match and screams at the garden, "If you do not grow, I will burn you!"

A gust of wind blows by and carries a tiny flame onto a dry withered stem. Within seconds the whole dead garden goes up in flames. The flames begin to spread to the gardener's house and soon after, the garden and the gardener's house have been burnt to a crisp.

After the fire department comes to extinguish the flames, they ask what caused this massive fire. The gardener explains that a tiny flame started the fire and the fire spread too fast to be put out by one person. The fire department smells the strong scent of gasoline and asks where the smell is coming from.

The gardener snarks, "Probably from my no-good dumb garden. I fed it everyday gasoline and sugar and it never once grew anything for me."

Bewildered, the fire department asks, "Why in the world would you feed your garden gasoline and sugar? Don't you know a garden needs water, not gasoline to grow? Gasoline will kill any plant right away."

The gardener is dumbfounded by this new information and then taken to jail for arson. The moral of this story, what you don't know can kill you or endanger you and others around you. Living a lie never produces the kind of fruits you would hope to gain. Had the gardener known the truth about what the garden actually needed, it would have saved them a lot of time and stress.

Truths are concepts and realities that are proven to be true time and time again, until infinity. Truths cannot be altered, for if they are altered, they are no longer true, but a lie. Laws provide order. Laws are meant to protect. Laws should be based on truth.

There are many universal laws that govern this world, such as the law of gravity, the law of gender, the law of vibration, the law of polarity, and the law of attraction. These laws help explain why everything in our world functions as it is supposed to. By understanding these laws, you can use them to your benefit and the universe. However, understanding the universal laws is not the point of this chapter. What I hope for you to gain in this chapter is a better understanding of what *truth* is. Why truth never fades. And why we need truth to live the life we were destined to live.

The following are The Laws of Truth that I live my life by. Many of these concepts I learned by reading the Bible. No matter your religious belief, I implore you to keep reading as these Truths are as practical as they are spiritual and can drastically change your life.

TRUTH #1
As A Man Thinks In His Heart, So Is He.

As a man thinks in his heart, so is he is a phrase that has been used in many self-help books and speeches. However, this phrase can be first found in the Bible and was written around 700 BC. This wise phrase states that whatever you think or believe in your mind to be true will become your reality. If you think in your mind that you cannot do a certain task, then your body will agree with you.

If you think you are worthless and incapable of being loved, your body will believe it also. You will put yourself in situations that can endanger you and distance you from being loved. If you choose to think the opposite, that you are priceless and capable of loving others and being loved by others, you will see your circle change. You will treat people differently, and you will notice people will treat you more favorably as well. It is important to control our thoughts because they can become our reality. If we choose to believe the wrong thoughts our lives can be misguided.

A negative thought, even in private, will eventually become your belief. If you constantly tell yourself that everyone gets promoted but me, that will affect your reality. You will see everyone around you getting promoted and moving up the ladder. You yourself may have worked for the company for ten years and still hold an entry-level position. The problem always seems to be everyone else; management is biased, this person is more educated, or that person is a flirt. You may believe you are the only hard worker and have nothing to show for all your hard work.

Do you realize how that type of attitude can affect your work performance? You spend all your energy despising the people around you, leaving you stagnating and miserable. To get promoted, it is better to switch your thinking to what you can do better.

Have you told your supervisor about your career desires? Have you asked what areas you need improvement in? After receiving the feedback, were you diligent in doing what was requested? Are you a joy to be around? Do you add value to an area of the business that is unmatched? Do you encourage others around you?

The problem is rarely external but rather internal. If we can eliminate the negative thoughts that plague our minds, we can free up space to let the positive flow. It only takes one positive thought for you to grasp and hold on to that can change your life.

To get you started, below are a few positive thoughts:

"I am capable of all things."

"I have a gift to share with the world."

"I can finish whatever I set my mind to."

"I am a leader."

"I can get my family out of debt."

"I can graduate college."

"I can start a business."

"I can get married."

"I can have children."
"I will live to be 120 years old."
"I can invent the next big thing."
"I am lovely and worthy to be loved."

TRUTH #2

Ask And You Shall Receive.

Growing up, the hardest thing I had to learn was that if I did not ask for what I wanted, I rarely got it. I assumed people knew what I wanted and would become frustrated when I did not get my way. However, I never considered that I did not ask for anything. Because I did not ask for anything and assumed the other person knew my needs, I had to accept what the other person gave me. It was not until I learned that most people are not mind-readers and if I did not ask for what I wanted, I would not get it.

As a kid, this happened often to me around Christmas time. I rarely asked for what I wanted for Christmas because I wanted to be surprised. However, after years of disappointing pajama gifts, I decided to ask for what I wanted so that I would no longer be surprised by my underwhelming gift.

This truth can also be broken down into the simplest terms of asking a question. In school, people sometimes feel embarrassed to raise their hands and ask questions. They do not want to look stupid or uncool by actively participating. When I first started my education journey, I too wanted to be accepted and cool, so I did not ask questions, even when the teacher asked, "Does anyone have any questions?"

I was silently screaming in my mind, "Yes! I have a question; please just answer it. Don't make me raise my hand." My fear of asking a question led me to lean on my own interpretation of what the teacher was teaching. My interpretations were often wrong, and the evidence was in my test results.

It was when I learned, "Ask and you shall receive" that I got the courage to raise my hand. I needed answers and couldn't wait any longer to receive the answers to my questions. Once I asked the teacher my question, I found that others around me had the same question. The teacher would even thank me for asking my question so that she had an opportunity to clarify for the whole class. My test results improved because my understanding was clear. The other students around me then began to notice and ask me for help with their homework and assignments.

Before I knew it, I was a question-asking fool! I loved asking questions. I would ask even if I knew the answer. It just felt better to know than to wonder; soon after, I was helping many of the students in my class with their assignments.

Ask and you shall receive. Ask not and you receive not.

TRUTH #3

God Will Allow What You Allow, But God Will Not Allow What You Do Not Allow.

This is one of my favorite scriptures in the Bible because it demonstrates the power that we human beings have on this Earth. God gave mankind the ability to create and do whatever comes to their minds. Many people do not know the power that they possess. They believe certain circumstances are out of their control and things are just the way they are. This is far from the truth. If we believe that we can do something, we can make it come to life in the real world. Most people lack the discipline to see their ideas through to the end.

When God created the world, he put in it everything mankind was going to need to sustain itself. The most important contribution God gave to mankind was our ability to use our minds to create and change our lives. What we decide to do with our minds is up to us.

If we decide we want to jump off a bridge, God says, "Go ahead; it's your God-given right."

If we decide to change our sexual orientation, God says, "Go ahead; it's your God-given right."

If we decide to end world hunger, God says, "Go ahead; it's your God-given right."

Now God may disapprove of some of our choices, but it is our God-given right. If we allow it, God will allow it. If we do not allow it, God will not allow it.

I have seen people questioning how God could allow tragedy. The question they should be asking is how could they or we allow this tragedy? What actions were witnessed and ignored prior to the tragedy? Could one conversation have changed the course of history?

If gangs and drug use overrun your neighborhood and you have sat idle and only complained about it, nothing will change. If you say, this street will be drug-free and gang-free that produces action. If you are serious, you will seek ways to rid your street of gangs and drugs. God is not going to move unless you do. Why should God care about your street if you don't even care for your own street?

Let's take it a little higher. If the doctor tells you that you have cancer, you have two options:

Option 1: Accept that you have cancer and allow it to grow in your body.

Option 2: Thank the doctor for finding the cancer and tell the cancer that you are not allowed to grow in my body. Moreover, cancer, you will dissolve out of my body and down the toilet.

I have read and heard miraculous stories of healing and transformation because people didn't allow their present circumstance to become their future. We have to speak up for ourselves and cancel some things out. We cannot continue to accept whatever the world wants to throw at us. It is our God-given right to have health and prosperity. It is up to us to exercise our rights or relinquish them.

TRUTH #4

Wisdom Is The Principal Thing, Therefore Get Wisdom. And In All Your Getting, Get Understanding. He Who Is Missing Wisdom Despises His Neighbor, But A Man of Understanding Holds His Peace.

Wisdom is different from knowledge. Knowledge is information. Wisdom is the ability to think and act using knowledge, experience, understanding, common sense, and insight. I think the keyword in the definition of wisdom is understanding. If you do not understand an issue, you cannot offer any wisdom or guidance to a person.

Suppose your neighbor drinks often and gets belligerent to the point of harming others. Most people's first thought is to put him in rehab or let him drink himself to death. A person acting with wisdom will seek to understand why the neighbor drinks so heavily and becomes abusive. Out of genuine care, the wise person gets to know the neighbor on a personal level. The neighbor opens up about his traumatic past in the military as a foot soldier. Every night he is haunted by dreams of him on the battlefield. He drinks until he blacks out so that he can sleep without dreams.

Now that we understand why the neighbor drinks so much, we can help him appropriately. Without understanding, you may despise your neighbor for his drunken ways. Understanding a person first allows you to put your judgemental emotions aside and empathize with the individual. You may not have the knowledge to help your neighbor with his drinking problem, but because you attempted to understand, you can have peace towards him and not hate.

This truth also applies to the ways of the world. Imagine someone panicking every night that the sun is gone. They even go as far as calling 911 and Homeland Security to report that the sun has been stolen. Knowledge of the Earth's rotation helps explain why the sun rises every day in the east and sets in the west. If we understand that concept, we will use wisdom and not panic when the sun sets and the Earth is turned into its nightly darkness.

Wisdom is the principal thing; therefore, get wisdom. And in all your getting, get understanding. He who is missing wisdom despises his neighbor, but a man of understanding holds his peace.

TRUTH #5

Hatred Stirs Up Strife, But Love Covers All Transgressions.

Do you have that one person at work that you just cannot stand? I mean, every time you see them your whole demeanor changes. Your heart starts to race and the hairs on the back of your neck stand straight up. You avoid eye contact or go out of your way to glare intently down their soul. If their name gets brought up, you automatically roll your eyes and say something to tarnish their image.

This is hatred in motion and it only stirs up strife. With all these negative emotions towards this person, you only see what they are doing wrong. Your judgment will become clouded and you will make decisions on an emotional level rather than doing the right thing.

Hitler let his hatred toward Jewish people lead him down the path of genocide.

A rabbi in the 13th Century single-handedly disrupted the natural way the Earth was operating by teaching people the truth of their existence and the truth of the world around them. Upon establishing this new nation, he gave laws that would govern humanity henceforth. The law was simple, Love God with all your heart, soul, and mind. Love your neighbor as you love yourself.

If we are to love the Creator, we have to focus our minds on acting according to his nature. If we are to love our neighbors as we love ourselves, we must first love ourselves. You cannot give someone a love that you have not experienced yourself. If the love you know is basic, surface level, and short-standing, you will give that same level of love to someone else.

If we do not know how to love, we will begin to abuse one another, distrust one another, and potentially kill one another. Love is a sacrificial decision to be kind, show courtesy, understand before trying to be understood, and forgive time after time.

The love a father has for his child should be forever. Although people may try, we cannot separate ourselves from the ones who brought us into this world spiritually or physically. The love we receive or the lack of love we receive from our fathers will determine how sturdy the foundational structure of our life is. We need love to function. Not superficial, "Oh, I love your outfit." Real love that stays. Love that is committed to love even when it becomes seemingly unbearable. The world is scattered with people needing love and making wrong decisions in an effort to find love.

If we can learn to love people for people with their differences, we can see that we are not much different. Everyone is fighting to preserve their family or their legacy. What is a legacy worth if it is built on hatred towards another group of people?

We are the Human Race and if we do not focus on preserving our own existence, we will continue to kill each other for the Glory of a few.

Hatred stirs up strife, but love covers all transgressions.

TRUTH #6

He Who Keeps Instruction Finds The Way of Life, But He Who Refuses Correction Will Go Astray.

This is a truth that I am still mastering. In essence, this truth is saying be coachable. We have to be taught and corrected if we are to be successful in this life. Growing up, I always thought I was smarter than the average person, even toward those that were older than me. This made it difficult for anyone to be able to teach me anything. I was a person who preferred to learn on my own or learn by experience. This led me to learn hard lessons on my own and time wasted. The great thing about having a coach, mentor, or parent is that they already had many of the experiences you will encounter. So you can skip a couple of steps by listening and heeding the words of your coach.

Here is a secret...life does not change much. If you are having relationship problems, those same problems existed back in ancient times and in the times of your grandparents and parents. Just because we ourselves are experiencing it for the first time does not mean this is the first time in history a situation like yours has arisen.

A loving father will teach his son how to swing a baseball bat. Suppose the child wants to hold the bat upside down and grip the fatter side of the baseball bat. The son believes by holding the bat in this manner he will hit more home runs. The child can swing his heart out to hit the ball and most likely miss every time. A wise son would listen when his father instructs him to flip the bat over and grip the narrow side. This will allow the son to have a better grip on the bat and he will also have a bigger surface for the baseball to make contact with.

A wise son will listen when their father corrects the way they are standing. A wise son will follow his father's instructions and allow his father to correct him when he is wrong. The father does this out of love for his son because he wants him to be great and have fun with the sport. Instruction and correction are necessary for improvement and growth.

Suppose the child did not listen to their father and kept swinging the bat upside down. I assume his fingers would get red, swollen, and filled with splinters over time. The child may now hate the sport of baseball and vow to never pick up a bat again.

He who keeps instruction finds the way of life, but he who refuses correction will go astray.

TRUTH #7

When Pride Comes, Then Comes Shame; But With The Humble Is Wisdom.

We hear so much about having pride in one's country, pride in oneself, or pride in your school. Our parents tell us that they are proud of us when we do a good job. At my high school, we would shout, "Tiger Pride!" from the stadium bleachers.

If we do something that appears foolish, people say, "Don't you have any pride! Where is your shame?"

So I was very surprised to learn that pride is not a good quality to have. Think of it this way; how many times has your "pride" stopped you from doing something?

"My pride wouldn't let me apologize, so I lost my job." Or "My pride kept me from saying what I should have said." Or "I am too prideful to do that type of work."

With pride comes shame. You later feel ashamed that you could not put your pride aside and be vulnerable. You regret the decision not to apologize. You regret not telling that person you love them too. You regret not humbling yourself to take that job with less pay.

Pride is like a superhero thinking he can take on all the bad guys in the world by himself. Sure, he may have slayed them all once before individually, so why would he need anyone else? So the superhero assumes he can slay all of them again by himself.

When the battle begins to look grim and the advantage is given to the bad guys, the superhero can call his other superhero buddies for help. However, the superhero feels he has an image to uphold and does not want to look weak. So he calls no one and, in the end, is defeated. Had the superhero humbled himself, he would have made the wise choice to call his friends for help and possibly one the battle.

Pride will keep you from asking for help. Pride will keep you from taking a risk. Pride will keep you from the life you are supposed to live. Find wisdom in being humble and vulnerable. It is those moments when you put your ego aside and are not afraid to look a little foolish.

I cannot tell you how many times I decided to be vulnerable with someone and it worked out better than I had expected. Yes, I was a little nervous about sharing an intimate secret or thought I had, but I knew if I didn't share, I would regret it.

The following story is not one of those times.

In high school, I played volleyball and loved the game. My little sister saw my passion for the game and decided she wanted to learn also. I began coaching her and practicing with her in our backyard. She became quite good and quickly became a great player. In middle school, she was one of the best players and by the time she came to high school, she was a force to be reckoned with.

I on the other hand, was an average, ok player. I loved the game, it kept me in shape, and I had fun doing it. I knew I wasn't that good, but it did not matter at the time. That all changed when my sister came to high school. I was two grades ahead of her and because of my playing skills, I thought I was destined to be a junior on the JV team. I was confident that my sister, as an incoming freshman, would either be on the JV team or Varsity.

Most people would love the opportunity to play with their siblings, but for me, it was a reflection of how basic I was. My little sister, the one I had coached, would be either playing with me or above me. My pride would not allow me to face my potential embarrassment, so I decided not to try out that year. I never stepped on the court again in a regulated game.

At the time, I told everyone that I did not like the coaching staff and I just didn't want to play the game anymore. But that was a lie. I was actually embarrassed that my little sister was better than me.

To my surprise, after tryouts, my sister was placed on the Freshman squad because they needed a strong player like her to uplift the team. I quit for no reason. I felt foolish and ashamed that I quit the sport I loved on the assumption that my little sister would be on my team. And even more foolish and ashamed of my reasoning. I should have been excited for my sister and ecstatic that we would have the opportunity to play together in a real game. However, because of my pride, I never got that opportunity.

Pride leads to regret and shame. Humbleness provides wisdom and acceleration to your goal.

TRUTH #8

A Fool's Wrath is Known At Once, But A Prudent Man Covers His Shame.

Slow to anger and quick to understand. This truth in essence, states that a person who reacts quickly without thinking will be put to shame. A person that acts with care of how his actions will be received is wise and is not put to shame.

Have you ever been around someone that lives by the code #nofilter? These people I would consider fools because they think without taking the time to care about how their response will impact themselves and others around them. They think it is cute or funny to say whatever they feel without regard for how it will be received. This person finds joy in putting other people in their "place". This person lacks self-restraint and is ruled by their emotions, not their intelligent mind. Another fool will follow this person's action to great detriment to themselves.

A filter is put in place to prevent toxic and dirty materials from entering the ecosystem. A car uses an air filter to purify the air coming into the car. Its basic function is to clean the air that circulates through your heating and cooling system. Filters trap and hold many types of particulates and contaminants that could affect your health and comfort. When we speak without a filter, we are letting whatever vile and harsh beliefs we have come out into the open air contaminating our environment.

Consider this story:

A great Queen calls in her two highest advisors to assist her with a matter of great importance. She received a tip that one of her advisors was a traitor and had been conspiring against the Kingdom with foes from another kingdom far away. The Queen was as wise as she was beautiful and decided to test the two advisors to see which one was the traitor. The Queen called both advisors to her chamber and spat on both of their faces without warning.

The first man fell to his feet, bowed to the Queen, and asked, "Oh Queen, in what manner have I offended you? Please forgive me for my transgression."

The second man was abruptly offended and yelled insults to the Queen, "You lowly pig, how dare you disgrace me with your bodily fluids! Get off the floor fool; she is no respectable Queen!"

When the second man finished his statement, the Queen had her guards come in and execute the man on the spot. She walked over to the bowing man and told him to rise. The Queen then explained her actions to her living advisor.

"Faithful and trustworthy advisor, please forgive me for spitting on you; it was a test. I had received word that one of my advisors was a traitor and to find out who it was, I had to do something not Queen-like. A fool's wrath is known at once, but a prudent man covers his shame. I will increase your position in the Kingdom for your faithfulness and give you more riches than you can spend in this lifetime."

It is not easy to hold your composure when someone has offended you, this I know. But it is better to hold your composure and still show respect for the individual that has offended you. Often by not getting rattled by an offense, the offender has to question themselves and their approach.

Contain your wrath and be wise with your words. Many people say mean and hurtful things when they are upset. Words they would never say if there was peace. They later regret their actions and have to work overtime to convince the other party that they did not mean what they had said. Save yourself the trouble and heartache. Excuse yourself until you can speak peacefully to that person. It is better to do this than to say something you will regret.

A fool's wrath is known at once, but a prudent man covers his shame.

TRUTH #9

You Reap What You Sow.

Everyone is responsible for what they plant or sow in the world. If you plant a sunflower seed, you will reap a sunflower stalk in the future. If you pour gasoline into your garden you will reap dead plants and dry soil. The Earth was meant to operate on the basis of sowing and reaping and not just buying and selling. There are many things that a person can sow. A person can sow into their minds good philosophy or bad philosophy. A person can sow double cheeseburgers into their body or vegetables into their body. A person can sow seeds of kindness or seeds of hatred. A person can sow whatever they choose, but whatever they sow, they will reap the harvest of it. This truth works both negatively and positively and it works the same for everyone.

This law can also be interpreted as you get out what you put in. If you desire to lose weight, you have to make a plan to do physical activity at least three times a week and eat the right types of food. If you are diligent and consistent in seeing your plan through in a matter of weeks, you will see the results you have desired.

Now the opposite.

If you desire to lose weight and make a plan to do physical activity at least three times a week and eat the right foods, but instead do no physical activity and eat burgers and chips in the weeks that follow, you will see the results of your decision on the scale, in your face, and around your waist. You get out what you put in. You reap what you sow.

Do not expect your circumstances to change if you have not changed what you are doing. You cannot get upset that your sunflower seed grew to be a sunflower stalk. That is what you planted! If you want a tomato, better plant some tomato seeds.

TRUTH #10

Do Not Only Be A Hearer, But A Doer.
Without Doing, You Will Have No Results.

The Bible talks about not being only a hearer of the Word but also a doer. A person cannot listen their whole lives and expect they can apply the same laws by listening. This just is not the case. Hearing and doing go hand in hand. The point of every test a teacher has ever given a student is to see if they can apply the lesson they taught. Can they do what they heard the teacher teach?

This truth is so important for everyone reading this to grasp. Do not only be a hearer of the word but a doer. This pertains to instructions, and teachings, and is true no matter your religion.

You have two ears and two eyes for a reason. And you have two arms and two legs for a reason. The ears and eyes are for you to see and hear what is possible. Your arms and legs are there to help you do the possibilities you have seen and heard. Use the full body to its maximum potential, and you will never be dissatisfied.

It benefits you little to read this book if you do not exercise a single concept out of it. Hearing without doing produces zero results. What is it worth to have a great idea if you do nothing with it? The world is filled with people that never acted on their genius ideas. Do not be one of them.

You can read all the self-help books you want, go to every business seminar, listen to a ton of sermons or podcasts, and yet if you do not put any of the advice you received into action, your business or your life will still be stagnant and you have no one to blame but yourself. That may sound harsh, but it is reality. Without doing, you will have no results. You cannot sit on the couch and wish the tv would change channels; you have to get up and turn the channel.

Do not only be a hearer, but a doer. Without doing, you will have no results.

TRUTH #11

If You Can Think It, You Can Do It.

Writing this book is evidence that if you can think it, you can do it. I have long contemplated writing *Have We Learned Anything Yet?* The idea had been swirling around in my head for years; it took for me to learn this truth and the previous truth for me to put my ideas on paper.

The mind is a marvelous thing; it can produce some wild and amazing images. The mind-blowing part of the mind is that if it can be seen in your thoughts, it can become real in your hands and before your eyes. The world is filled with people who think and have done.

- Mahatma Gandhi visualized in his mind an India free from British rule and it became real before his eyes.
- Bill Gates visualized in his mind every family having a personal computer and it became real before his eyes.
- Harriet Tubman visualized herself freeing countless slaves from southern slave owners and it became real before her eyes.

With enough determination and discipline to see your ideas all the way through, you can think and do whatever comes to your mind. This truth is also positive and negative. Not every thought we have is a good one or conducive to life. You can think of killing someone and you can do that as well. I do not endorse murder whatsoever, but we have to discuss both sides.

The point is that we have the ability to create in reality the ideas that are in our minds. The book you are currently reading was in my mind and now it is on paper for you to read. As I sat here and typed each letter, I was transferring my thoughts to reality. You can do the same.

I suggest writing your ideas down on paper. That will help you visualize what you are thinking. Once your idea is on paper, this is a great time to decide whether this is a good idea or a bad idea. Not all ideas are equal in weight. Not all ideas are purposed for the time when it was thought of. Thinking happens fast; doing takes more time. Doing requires people, resources, and a stick-to-it mentality. The journey happens in the doing and not necessarily in the thinking. We need both to move us forward. If you can discipline yourself to see your good ideas all the way through, you will be rewarded and achieve your desires.

If you can think it, you can do it!

HAVE WE LEARNED ANYTHING YET?

Which of these laws were you already living by? Which of these truths will you apply to your life?

6

Eagles and Chickens: You are What You Believe

There once was an eagle who thought he was a chicken. When the eagle was very young, he fell from the safety of his nest. A chicken farmer found the eagle, brought him to his farm, and raised him in a chicken coop among his many chickens. Soon the eagle began behaving like a chicken. He walked like a chicken, clucked like a chicken, ate what chickens ate, and thoroughly believed he was a chicken.

Word spread around town that a three-foot-tall, seven-foot wingspan eagle was walking, moving, and eating like a one-foot-tall chicken. One day, an ornithologist or bird scientist came to the chicken farm to see if the rumors were true about an eagle believing he was a chicken. From his experience studying birds, he knew that eagles are the king of the sky, a carnivore, and one of the largest birds of prey.

To his astonishment, when he got to the farm, the eagle was strutting around the chicken coop, pecking at the ground, and acting very much like a chicken. The farmer explained to the scientist that this bird was no longer an eagle. He was now a chicken because he had been trained to be a chicken his whole life and the eagle now believed that he was, in fact, a chicken. The farmer told the scientist that the eagle didn't even know he could fly.

The scientist knew there was more to this great bird than his actions and current beliefs about itself. The eagle was born an eagle, had the heart of an eagle, and nothing could change that. The man lifted the eagle onto the fence surrounding the chicken coop and said, "Eagle, thou art an eagle. Stretch forth thy wings and fly." The eagle tilted its head in curiosity at this peculiar man. He then glanced down at his home among the chickens in the chicken coop, jumped off the fence, and resumed clucking around the coop.

The farmer was satisfied. "I told you it was a chicken," he said.

The scientist, however, was not satisfied. He returned the next day and tried again to convince the farmer and the eagle that the eagle was born for something greater. He took the eagle to the top of the farmhouse and spoke to it saying, "Eagle, thou art an eagle. You belong to the sky and not to the earth. Stretch forth thy wings and fly!"

The large bird looked at the man, then again down into the chicken coop. The eagle jumped off from the man's arm onto the roof of the farmhouse and shuffled back down to the ground with his chicken family.

The scientist asked the farmer to let him try one more time. The scientist was persistent; he understood the nature of an eagle and its capabilities. He was determined to return the next day and prove that this bird was an eagle.

The farmer laughed, shook his head, and said, "It is a chicken, but sure come back tomorrow and try again!"

The scientist returned the next morning to the chicken farm and took the eagle and the farmer some distance away to the peak of a high mountain. None of them could see the farm nor the chicken coop from this high place. The man held the eagle out in his arms and pointed high into the sky where the bright sun was beaming from above.

He spoke to the bird, "Eagle, thou art an eagle! You belong to the sky and not to the earth. Stretch forth thy wings and fly!" This time the eagle stared skyward into the bright sun, straightened his large body, and stretched his massive wings. His wings flapped hesitant at first, then with each thrust, more sure and more powerful. Then alas, with a mighty screech of an eagle, the bird lifted itself and flew up and through the sky.[56]

HAVE WE LEARNED ANYTHING YET?

Are you living like a chicken but are really an eagle? How can you find out? How do we discover our purpose in this life? Why were we brought here and what are we supposed to do with all of our time? The eagle was lucky; some random scientist came by and straightened him right up. But what if nobody came for the eagle? Would the eagle be stuck living like a chicken his whole life or would he eventually figure it out?

The best way I found to live in my purpose is to do what comes naturally to me. I developed my strength in the skills that came naturally to me. I used those skills to help others by adding value to their company or situations. For instance, organizing colors and shapes in my head come naturally to me. I have used that strength to organize clothing arrangements and displays at major department stores across the Midwest. Because my skills are valuable, leaders have sought me out to create impactful moments in their departments and stores. By using my skills, I am working on my purpose. The further I can develop my organizational skills and apply them to more trades or industries, the further I can grow in my purpose.

What came naturally to the eagle was to fly and hunt from the sky. However, the eagle had to develop confidence and leave convenience to align itself with its nature. I believe even though the scientist took the eagle up the mountain and told him his potential it was still up to the eagle to believe it.

What if the scientist was lying? What if he really was a chicken and was about to fall to his unfortunate death? I believe that deep down, the eagle knew he was destined for something greater. He just couldn't see his way out of the coop he was in. Sometimes you need a fresh perspective for you to realize what you already knew and become who you were created to be.

A lot can be learned from the eagle and the chicken. What I took away from this peculiar fable is that:

1. You are what you believe.
2. Your potential is locked inside of you and waiting for you to act on it.
3. Sometimes change requires a change in scenery.
4. Your nature determines your purpose

TRANSFERRING ENERGY

Did you know just by thinking about being late to an event can cause energy and actions to attract what you feared?

Same as you believing you are coming into a large fortune, you can attract money your way?

The world operates on energy. Every life form is entangled in an endless transaction of energy exchange. The entire world benefits from the release of the energy provided by our fauna friends. Plants receive energy from the sun to grow, which is then released into the atmosphere in the form of oxygen. Oxygen-breathing life forms absorb the energy from the plants and, in exchange, release carbon dioxide back to the plants. This is one of the simplest forms of how energy is exchanged on this planet. But it is not the only form.

The energy transferred from the flower exists even if we don't feel it like a disappointed relative or a pleased mother. Some energy doesn't need any exertion of force. It can be felt and absorbed based on its pure strength!

Have you ever been around someone who is having a bad day? Did you notice that the more they continue to talk, the worse you feel? Even after they walk away, you feel anxious, tense, and tired. The next person you talk to will now feel that same energy. That's negative energy at work. This type of energy produces undesirable results and can cause complacency, anxiety, stress, depression, narcissism, and lower self-esteem.

What if you could control the energy you receive and decide how to channel it? By studying electrical energy, one may find a clue as to how to transfer or repurpose energy. In electrical engineering, three elements are at work to guide energy. Those elements are conductors, insulators, and resistors[57].

A conductor allows energy to flow easily through itself to its endpoint. The conductor is simply the guide and provides little to no resistance to the energy flowing through it. This reduces the loss of energy in the transfer process. An insulator is used to reduce or split the transfer of energy. Insulators are used to protect the energy flowing from the environment or protect the environment from the energy. *It is a key safety measure.* Resistors are components that slow down the current in the circuit. Resistors deliberately lose energy to repurpose the energy in another form.

How does this relate to humans? Is it possible for us to control or manipulate energy? Can we be conductors and guide energy, so we are not only victims of it?

Think of a train conductor as the conductor of energy. The train conductor's job is to make sure the transfer of customers from stop to stop is done efficiently and with little to no margin of error. The most powerful form of energy the conductor possesses is his words. Through the power of his words, he has to assemble, coordinate, and direct passengers, in addition to communicating with the crew, groundskeepers, and rail traffic controllers.

It is in the best interest of the conductor to have a solid system in place to guide his energy to keep the train on schedule. One mishap could delay the train, derail the train, or send the train in the wrong direction. The safety measures of insulators or, in this example, train attendants and rail traffic controllers are put into place to prevent the flow of misinformation to the train conductor. Miscommunications cause resistance and can transfer into the form of delays, angry customers, or confusion. If all of the energy is properly guided, the conductor can ensure the passengers arrive safely to their destination.

Now place yourself at your favorite music group's concert or your favorite theatre performance. The performer in this example is electricity and the audience is the conductor. The electrical energy from the performer needs somewhere to transfer to. Assuming the energy transfer is pleasurable, the audience receives the energy from the performer easily and guides the electricity through their bodies and into the atmosphere in the form of singing, shouting, dancing, laughing, or clapping.

Another example is the spread of knowledge. As an educator, the job requires teachers to transfer the knowledge they possess to their pupils. Any teacher reading this may say that the transfer of knowledge is not easy and can be filled with tons of resistance. In a perfect world, all teachers would be *SUPERCONDUCTORS!* A superconductor always receives zero to no resistance in its energy transfers. Allowing smooth transfers of energy or, in this case, knowledge.

A resistor can cause delays and confusion in a situation. Think of the resistor as the Class Clown. It does not matter how hard the teacher tries to get the class on the same page and conduct the energy; the Class Clown will deliberately resist and slow the learning process.

There are also insulators at work to divide energy flow to certain power sources. An example of this is Jim Crow laws that were put in place in southern American states to prevent Black Americans from getting an equal education for fear that once educated Black Americans would rebel. So to keep the energy flowing in the south's favor, insulators were put in place to divert power away from Black Americans. Or fast forward to today where many women in nations worldwide are still fighting for equal opportunity to receive an education like their male counterparts. Insulator laws are put in place to keep women uneducated and powerless.

As humans, we have zero power in creating energy, but we have a choice in how the energy we receive or emit will flow or transfer. Humans are the only species on the planet that have this ability. All other species are merely vessels that are controlled by circumstances and physical abilities. Humans have the power to decide, choose, accept, reject, change, and create with our minds. Being aware of your power frankly gives you power.

BELIEFS IN ACTION

The story of the eagle and the chicken reminds me of another story that I read in the book, *The Richest Man in Babylon by* George S. Clason[58]. At the beginning of the story, there was a man named Bansir who was living in poverty. He is in the process of building a golden chariot that, upon completion, would increase his wealth. However, Bansir is unmotivated to complete the chariot even though completing it would bring him much-needed income and allow him to provide food for his family. It's in this moment of wallow that a good friend of his by the name of Kobbi stops by and, upon seeing Bansir relaxing on the side of the road, asks for two shekels.

Bansir shares with Kobbi that if he gave him two shekels, that would be all the money he has and that a wise man does not give all he owns to anyone, not even his good friend. Bansir goes on to describe a dream in which he was a man of much means. His fortune knew no end; he was fortunate enough to give money carelessly to beggars and decorate his wife with the most precious of jewels. Kobbi agrees that this is indeed a good dream and if he desires wealth, he should ask the richest man in Babylon how he acquired his wealth.

The richest man in Babylon was a man named Arkad. Arkad grew up with Bansir and Kobbi; he went to the same school as them, played the same games, and lived in the same village. But yet, he is now so rich that even the King seeks his wisdom. The men decided to ask Arkad his secret of how he became so wealthy.

When the men found Arkad they asked him, "How did fate pick Arkad to have great fortune? Did we not learn the same lessons when we were boys? Did we not play the same games? Did we not have the same teachers? Did we not live in the same village? If yes, to all of our questions, then why Arkad, has your life become so dramatically and lavishly different from ours?"

It is then that Arkad says something truly insightful.

"If you have not acquired more than a bare existence in the years that we were a youth, it is because you have either failed to learn the laws that govern wealth or you do not observe them." Arkad goes on to say, "I decided to myself that I would claim my share of the good things of this life. I would not become one of those who stand afar off enviously watching others enjoy. I would not be content clothing myself in the cheapest raiment that looked respectable. I would not be satisfied with the lot of a poor man. On the contrary, I would make myself a guest at the banquet of good things."

HAVE WE LEARNED ANYTHING YET?

Is it that easy to only decide to want something grand in life and be able to attain it? Does this rule apply to everyone or only a select chosen few? Can we be whatever we want to be?

Do we only have to believe or is there more to it? Would you believe it if you were told that you could be anything you wanted to be? Why is it so easy for a kid to believe they can do whatever they set their minds to? At what age do we give up fighting for our beliefs and conform to an average existence? Is average good enough?

How do we move beliefs into action?

Bob Proctor, a world-renowned speaker, motivational coach, and bestselling author of his book "You Were Born Rich" teaches the Law of Attraction[59] and how to bring out the potential from within you. Proctor gives a wonderful example of how to produce results from oneself by altering one's paradigm. In one of his teachings, he explained how the mind works.

Take, for example, a thought; as humans, we think over a million thoughts a day. Thoughts can be either negative or positive. When a thought comes into one's mind, an individual can either accept those ideas or reject them. If they choose to reject their thought, the thoughts immediately exit the mind and cause the body not to move on to that thought. If they choose to accept that thought, the thought drops into a person's paradigm, or depository of beliefs, and causes the body to produce a result.

For example:

A thought comes into your mind and tells you that you're hungry. You agree and choose to accept this thought. Your body will get the message and produce signs of hunger such as stomach growling, mouth salivation, hunger headaches, and hangry attitudes. The next thought in your head is about a jelly-filled donut. This thought you ponder for a while. On one hand, jelly-filled donuts are always a good idea, but on the other, you have your fitness goals to consider. Ultimately you decide to reject this thought and like clockwork, you're on to the next thought about a second more healthier option. A Mediterranean salad comes to mind and you decide to accept this thought. Your body is put into motion to order your salad and the next thing you know it is in front of your face to enjoy. But what if you could take our thoughts further than deciding what's for lunch?

Growing up I frequently heard people saying, "You can be whatever you want to be."

"Dream BIG!"

"The world is yours to form!"

"You were put on this world for a reason."

And my favorite, "The Children are the Future!"

After many years of hearing this, I chose to follow everyone's advice and "Dream BIG!" I moved to a big city and became a brand ambassador for a major fashion brand. I thought by being in a major city, I would "make it" in no time. But I was soon to discover that I was a small speck of glitter in a pool of sand. Part of me believed that fate would kick in and things would just fall into place. And some of that may be true, but like with most situations in this life you have to choose a path and walk down it.

There are many ways to get what you want out of this life, but you must figure out the best path. That path can be straight, traditional, wild, adventurous, spontaneous, risky, short, long, quiet, or bold. However you live it, you have to choose. The lack of choice will cause circumstances to dictate how you live your life. I could not wait in my apartment and go to work every day and expect someone to notice my talents. I had to put myself in a position to get noticed. If I didn't, circumstances would decide my own fate.

How can we control our lives? How can we think of an idea and bring it forth? How do we become whatever we want to be? How do we fulfill that grandmaster plan set for our lives before the foundation of the world?

Over time, I became cynical and thought it was all quite frankly bullshit. People couldn't be whatever they wanted to be because life is real and often has a way of giving you a rude awakening. I believed the world system was rigged and only those with the right connections got anywhere. The nice guy finishes last if he even finishes.

As I advanced in age and took on more responsibilities, the dreams I once had as a child slowly began to dissolve. I could no longer envision myself living out these big dreams and expectations. I saw myself as an American pit bull in a middle-class home - comfortably living but not really amounting to my potential.

Like many others, I followed the path of the American Dream and went to college in pursuit of a degree to obtain that dream job that would one day help me pursue my mission in life. After four and a half years, I earned my Bachelor's degree. I was ready to take on the world with a degree in hand. I believe I have a Facebook post that says the exact same thing.

I had the highest expectations of what my life would be like in the next one to three years. I was going to have an important job at a fashion company making $50,000-$75,000 out the gate. I was going to have one of those cute loft apartments in New York City and have brunch every weekend with my new, very cool friends. Then reality came crashing in, and two months after graduation, I was moving back into my parent's house in Ohio.

I was not one of the lucky ones who had a job lined up for me after completing school. So here I was, living with my parents and scouring the internet for jobs. Yippee! I probably applied for 100 jobs and nothing was working out. I eventually found myself employed in the same line of work that I was doing in prior to college.

You can imagine my family's disappointment when they found out that the only person in our family that graduated from a four-year college was working retail, picking out outfits for customers, and cleaning fitting rooms. I found myself angry at myself and feeling stupid for paying for four years of college just to be making a quarter more than minimum wage.

It was also at this time that I made a decision. I was going to work this job, be the best I could be, make connections, stack my money, and move out to New York City in one year. So I put my head down, worked two jobs, networked, stood out, and BAM! A year from the date of my declaration, I was moving out! But not to New York City, but to the Windy City of Chicago.

Now let's be clear, not all of my problems were solved by moving to Chicago, but I did learn that this stuff actually does work. I could declare something, move my body to produce the results that I wanted, and have what I desired.

You may say, "Well she didn't make it to New York; she failed."

That is the thing about all of this; sometimes things go according to plan, and other times better than planned! Had I not made a plan to do well where I was working, I may never have seen the opportunity to get promoted to my dream city. I may have never left my parent's house.

I believe the plan for your life was laid out before you were born. When we begin to find and use the treasures in our minds we activate sections of the plan.

For me, the first treasure I had to find was the idea that I should live in a major city. Once I believed that I was led to an opportunity to work for a company that was building a new location in New York City. The next treasure I had to find was the idea that I could be promoted to that location in one year. When I believed that, I was promoted to an entry-level management position within six months. I set my sights on New York City, but as fate would have it, 6 months later, I was going to Chicago. Why?

I believe The Creator of the plan knows what will motivate you to move. For me moving to New York City was my motivation and that's what was used for my benefit. However, in the actual design, I was always meant to be in Chicago. As you begin to follow the treasure in your mind, you may find yourself in the most unlikely of situations. Things will not always go according to plan. But be persistent in your pursuit because once the dust settles, you are able to see that everything worked out better than planned.

> *Many are the plans in the mind of a man, but it is the purpose of the LORD that will stand.*
> *Proverbs 19:21 (ESV)*

Did you know that you can also curate what becomes true in your mind?

Jim Rohn[60] an entrepreneur, author, and motivational speaker, once said,

> "We have the total responsibility on how to live our lives, what direction we want to go in, the thoughts and ideas that come into our heads, and definitely the action needed to do things is totally up to us. The fact that we need to guard our thoughts and ideas that come

into our minds is a crucial one. It has been said that the most valuable space in the world is the six inches between our ears. Yet most people, including me, don't guard and protect that half a foot of space enough. It's never too late to post a guard to the entrance of our minds along with realizing the power of the things that go on in between our ears that affect our entire life."

As the author of your own story, you have the potential to create whatever you decide to bring forth from your mind. This ability was given to you by the Heavenly Creator. No other species on this earth can do it. All it requires is a little faith; faith, the size of a mustard seed, will do. Proctor states that people can alter their realities by altering their perception of being. This means that people can change their lives, and the reality around them if they first change their perception of themselves.

Will it be challenging? - Yes and No

The evil one or gem stealer, as I like to call him, is at work plotting ways to keep you in your slump and routine. He is after the gems in your mind. *How many golden ideas have you had that never came about? What stopped you? Did someone tell you it was a dumb idea? Did your family not support you?*

From my experience, these are tricks or thieves at work to rob you of your God-given treasures. When I was about to move to Chicago, people could not understand why I would want to move to the Murder Capital of the United States. A valid concern, but it wasn't their burden to bear. This was my decision and my decision alone. The desire, the idea, was not put in their hearts and because of that, their eyes could not see.

And let's be clear, it's no fault of your friends and family who don't quite get it or support it. People make decisions based on their perception of reality. Experiences from childhood or adulthood have a critical role in a person's beliefs and decision-making. What's right for one may not be right for another. What God has in store for me is different from what he has in store for you. But we all have something. And not just a little something... it's A LOT of something remarkable!

Just as the most valuable space in the world is the six inches between our ears, so is the biggest battle. In this increasingly digital and smaller world, everyone is fighting for your attention and your commitment. Uneducated and educated opinions are mixed and broadcast worldwide to vie for your loyalty. As people, we have to safeguard the gates to our minds and not let anything in that could cause our bodies to produce undesirable results. Gather your own factual information and form your own unique decision.

Let's also be clear that not all ideas are equal in value; similar to not all gems are equal in value. If you decide to jump off a bridge, most people would agree that's not a wise idea. But what if you decide to jump off a bridge and wear a bungee cord attached to a certified professional? Still Risky, but a much better idea.

Be honest with yourself about your ideas. Write them down so you can see what your mind is thinking. You may discover that your mind runs wild with all sorts of wonderful, strange, insane, and beautiful ideas.

We have the power to choose a different path than friends and family. The power to decide how we want to orchestrate our lives and how we want to live our life. The power to decide how much money we want to make, where we live, and who we associate with.

Life is the sum of numerous decisions and interactions. You may be one decision away from drastically changing your life. Do not fear; while the first step may feel lonely, the rest of the journey is full of friends to support you.

Will life continue to challenge you? - Absolutely YES!

But I believe if you train yourself to be consciously aware of your thoughts; what's coming in your mind, what you're acting on, what you choose to believe, and what you regard as foolish, you can change the outcome of your life.

The world is full of examples of individuals that had to break the mold and think a different thought than those of their inherited community. What was their secret? The secret is to think, decide, and take action on your ideas. As Proctor would say, If you can see it in your mind, you can hold it in your hand.

> *Therefore I say to you, whatever things you ask for when you pray, believe that you will receive them, and you will have them.*
> *Mark 11:24 (NKJV)*

7

Have You Learned Anything Yet?

By now, you've had some time to consider the stories, tales, and lessons written herein. This, my friends, is the final chapter. So, what do you believe?

Have we, mankind, learned anything yet? Have you learned anything yet about yourself? Will you learn more about our shared history? Will you learn to renew and use your mind to excite change? Will you continue to fight in wars? Will you create new and beautiful things? Have you learned about the cyclical nature of time? Will you repeat history? Will you seek to understand the truth? Will you exercise truth? Do you understand how to love? Will you choose to love?

This final chapter is one that you, the reader, will help write. Throughout this book, I have presented you with humanity's case. I have shown you mankind's story from the very beginning. I have shown you different ways ancient and modern societies have chosen to manage people and our resources. I have shown you what you are capable of if you believe. I also have shown you the horrors of what mankind is capable of as a whole.

At the beginning of this book, I told you that this is not a book of answers. This is a book of questions. This is a book written to humanity in search of answers.

What are we fighting for? Not only physically but as a collective mission. What is the goal that mankind is collectively working toward? Is it ending world hunger? Is it ending racial inequality? Is it about national power over other nations? Is it leaving Earth and traveling the stars?

Mankind has always fought in tribes. Some tribes have been much larger than others and have shaped our world. But if we know anything from history, all great nations collapse. The poor build and the wealthy create. The wealthy create the plan and the poor execute the plan. The wealthy collect the money and give it sparingly to the poor. This is how it has always been. Inequality is nothing new and does not pertain to skin color or national origin. We fail to acknowledge that both parties are equal in this current system.

What if we looked at the system differently and exchanged value for value? The creator is equal to the builder. Doesn't the builder need the creator to envision something for him to build? And doesn't the creator need the skilled work and passion of the builder to build his vision?

Neither one can exist without the other. Perhaps if we looked at each other in these terms, we could eliminate the illusion of power if we understand that without the builders, no city can become great and without creators, we would have nothing to look forward to. Perhaps we can learn from our past and create a better future. This is my hope for mankind, a collective focus. Languages and culture are invisible differentiators that mean nothing. Ultimately, every person wants to provide for their family and contribute something to this world. Why can't we do that together?

You may be familiar with the story of the Israelites from the ancient Jewish scriptures. According to the scriptures, in the early days of humanity, the descendants of Abraham's grandson, Jacob (whose name was later changed by God to Israel) was chosen to be God's favored people. These people became known as the Israelites. As the Israelite people multiplied and grew, some people became tainted and started to worship other gods. This displeased the Lord and because of the people's disobedience, God allowed the Israelites to be taken up as slaves to the Egyptians. The Israelites were enslaved by the Egyptians for over 400 years.

Because of the Israelites' cries, God raised a man named Moses, who was to be the savior of Israel, releasing the Israelites from the stronghold of the Egyptian Pharaoh. With the help of God's power, Moses unleashed numerous plagues upon Egypt. After many plagues and the heart-breaking loss of Pharoah's firstborn son, Pharoah released the Israelites from slavery in Egypt. Moses then led the Israelites away from the city and onward to God's promised land for them. However, along the journey, some of the people became impatient as the journey became longer and more challenging than expected. A journey that was supposed to take three weeks ended up taking forty years. The forty years is known as The Wilderness.

Eventually, after forty years of blessings and toil, the new generation of Israelites made it into God's promised land. However, the promised land was already taken by other individuals that were not Israelites and worshipped other gods. This led to another forty years of wars and battles before the Israelites were able to claim the land that was promised to them and dwell in it peacefully.

Many lessons can be learned from the story of the Israelites. One is that complaining gets you nowhere and can make any journey more difficult than it has to be. Two, just because something is promised to you does not mean it will come easy. Three, sometimes, after leaving a horrible situation, you have to go through a period of humbleness and shedding before you are able to reap the rewards of your sacrifices. And the fourth and final lesson is faith will only take you as far as your faith. Have we learned anything yet?

I believe the story of the Israelites is a story for all people; if you remove the names and heritage of the Israelites they were just people. People that had been treated unjustly and deserved better living and working conditions. People that were looking for a home in a world that had discounted them and moved on without them. People that left everything they had been accustomed to for generations in hopes of having a better life for their families and preceding generations.

Are we much different today? Every nation may have its own heritage, customs, culture, and spoken language, but at the end of the day, the goal is to come home and be with your family. We fight wars to protect our families and way of life; we work overtime at the job to provide for our families, and we spend countless hours teaching and correcting ourselves in hopes of having a better future. This is the story of mankind; this is the story of us all. We are not different; we are all the same. Fighting the same battles to achieve the same goals. We all want to be remembered after we leave this Earth. We want our lives to have meaning, to have an impact on the world, and to be remembered for many generations—all in the pursuit of adding a sentence, chapter, or section to the Book of Life.

My final questions to you, dear reader, are as follows:

What is the goal for the future of humankind? Should we have a collective focus that everyone in the world is striving to reach? Or should we continue to live as we always have, in small communities fighting to survive in our small tribes? Are we capable of anything more? Are we living to mankind's fullest potential? Can we set aside differences to achieve something totally new and unfathomable to the ancestors that came before us? Can we act as a single body working towards a worthy goal? Can we respect each other without any prejudices?

In my opinion, if mankind stays on the path or cycle that we are on, then by understanding the cyclical nature of history, we know what to expect in the future. The poor will strive to be wealthy and the wealthy will continue to distance themselves from the poor. Powerful nations will collapse from within and break off into smaller groups. War will occur every generation based on the desire to obtain more power. And lastly, history will continue to repeat with new faces and new players entering this ancient game, having similar outcomes as the generation before them. Is this the world we want to look forward to?

How this story ends is up to you. **Fill the remaining pages of this book with your thoughts and subsequent actions to my many questions.** Do you believe we have learned anything yet? Why or Why not? What will you do about it?

Dear friend, I pray this book was of some use to you, and one day we can meet so that you may share what you have learned with me.

Much Gratitude and Love,

K. R. Hawthorne

The Reader's Ending

These pages are here for you to answer the questions I have asked throughout this book. Have we learned anything yet? Do you believe we've learned anything yet from our ancestor's mistakes and triumphs? Why or Why not? What should we do to move all mankind forward into the next phase of our evolution?

Write your thoughts and actions to achieve your desired result. Refer to the **HAVE WE LEARNED ANYTHING YET?** sections throughout the chapters as your starting point.

Acknowledgements

To God be the Glory first and foremost. For without him, I am nothing.

To my husband, Dashawn, for believing that I could write a book and providing me with the opportunity to bring my dream to fruition.

Thank you.

To Michael Bart Mathews at We Create Books for mentoring me as I wrote and providing valuable feedback every step of the way.

Thank you.

To my crew of family and friends that helped edit my first and very rough draft of Have We Learned Anything Yet: Deron and Traci aka Papa and Mom, My dear brother David, Aunt Tami, Aunt Toni, Brittany, Joe, and Maggie (Xiaomin). Your support and feedback gave me some much-needed guidance.

Thank you.

And lastly, to you, the reader, for picking up this piece of literature and being curious. For still craving to read in a world of pictures and videos.

Thank you.

REFERENCES

1. Pennsylvania Society For Promoting The Abolition Of Slavery. An address to the public, from the Pennsylvania Society for promoting the abolition of slavery, and the relief of free negroes, unlawfully held in bondage ... Signed by order of the Society, B. Franklin, President. Philadelphia, 9th of November. Philadelphia, 1789. Pdf. Retrieved from the Library of Congress, <www.loc.gov/item/2005577131/>.
2. Holy Bible, New King James Version. The Gideons International, National Publishing Company, 1985
3. Johnson, B. (2011, August 17). The factor of faith in crime reduction. Chron. Retrieved April 18, 2021, from https://www.chron.com/opinion/outlook/article/The-factor-of-faith-in-crime-reduction-2079575.php.
4. Mark, J. (2020, December 18). Hammurabi. Retrieved December 21, 2020, from https://www.ancient.eu/hammurabi
5. Issues and Trends in China's Demographic History: Asia for Educators: Columbia University. (n.d.). Retrieved December 21, 2020, from http://afe.easia.columbia.edu/special/china_1950_population.htm
6. Nicholas, B. (1975). *An introduction to Roman law*. Oxford: Clarendon Press.
7. Law in Ancient Rome, The Twelve Tables. (n.d.). Retrieved December 21, 2020, from https://www.crystalinks.com/romelaw.html
8. Roman law. (2020, November 10). Retrieved March 08, 2020, from https://www.britannica.com/topic/Roman-law
9. Feature, 2. (2019, May 22). The Contribution of Roman Law to Modern Legal Systems. Retrieved December 21, 2020, from https://europeanconservative.com/2019/05/the-contribution-of-roman-law-to-modern-legal-systems/

10. Fercility. (2020, June 13). The Han Dynasty: History, Emperors, Events, Background. Retrieved August 21, 2020, from https://www.chinahighlights.com/travelguide/china-history/the-han-dynasty.htm
11. Hays, J. (n.d.). HAN DYNASTY ECONOMY. Retrieved December 21, 2020, from http://factsanddetails.com/china/cat2/sub2/entry-5427.html
12. Bulhan, H. A. (2015). Stages of Colonialism in Africa: From Occupation of Land to Occupation of Being. *Journal of Social and Political Psychology*, *3*(1), 239-256. https://doi.org/10.5964/jspp.v3i1.143
13. Williams, 1966 Williams, E. (1966). *Capitalism and slavery*. New York, NY, USA: Capricorn Books.
14. Rodney, 1974 Rodney, W. (1974). *How Europe underdeveloped Africa*. Washington, DC, USA: Howard University Press.
15. Jones, J. (2015, May 27). Emoji is dragging us back to the dark ages – and all we can do is smile. Retrieved December 21, 2020, from https://www.theguardian.com/artanddesign/jonathanjonesblog/2015/may/27/emoji-language-dragging-us-back-to-the-dark-ages-yellow-smiley-face
16. Edwin Starr; War(What is it Good For?) Album: War & Peace. Released: 1970
17. Wilson, E. O. (2013). The social conquest of Earth. Liveright Publ. Retrieved September 25, 2020, from http://www.ingramanthropology.com/uploads/6/8/1/1/6811328/wilson_is_war_inevitable.pdf.
18. Independent Digital News and Media. (2014, July 14). *Saharan remains may be evidence of first race war, 13,000 years ago*. The Independent. Retrieved May 21, 2020, from https://www.independent.co.uk/news/science/archaeology/saharan-remains-may-be-evidence-of-first-race-war-13000-years-ago-9603632.html.
19. Ferguson, R. (2018, September 1). War Is Not Part of Human Nature. Retrieved June 15, 2019, from https://www.scientificamerican.com/article/war-is-not-part-of-human-nature/
20. Mark, J. (2020, December 20). War in Ancient Times. Retrieved December 21, 2020, from https://www.ancient.eu/war/
21. War. Retrieved December 21, 2020, from https://www.merriam-webster.com/dictionary/war

22. Smedley Butler on Interventionism. (n.d.). Retrieved May 21, 2021, from https://fas.org/man/smedley.htm.
23. [Juhasz, A. (2013, April 15). *Why the war in Iraq was fought for big oil*. CNN. Retrieved August 15, 2020, from https://www.cnn.com/2013/03/19/opinion/iraq-war-oil-juhasz/index.html.
24. Cartwright, M. (2021, September 19). Persian wars. Ancient History Encyclopedia. Retrieved December 15, 2019, from https://www.ancient.eu/Persian_Wars/.
25. Cartwright, M. (2019, September 17). Delian League. Ancient History Encyclopedia. Retrieved August 15, 2020, from https://www.ancient.eu/Delian_League/.
26. United Nations. (n.d.). Maintain international peace and security. United Nations. Retrieved September 26, 2022, from https://www.un.org/en/our-work/maintain-international-peace-and-security
27. Morris, Ian. *War! What Is It Good For?: Conflict and the Progress of Civilization From Primates to Robots*. First edition. New York: Farrar, Straus and Giroux, 2014. Print.
28. Wikimedia Foundation. (2021, September 18). List of wars by death toll. Wikipedia. Retrieved December 28, 2020, from https://en.wikipedia.org/wiki/List_of_wars_by_death_toll.
29. Bangladesh population (LIVE). Worldometer. (n.d.). Retrieved August 3, 2020, from https://www.worldometers.info/world-population/bangladesh-population/.
30. *The Tainted Gift*; Barbara Alice Mann; ABC-CLIO; 2009; pp. 1–18
31. History.com Editors. (2010, October 12). Spanish flu. History.com. Retrieved December 19, 2020, from http://www.history.com/topics/1918-flu-pandemic.
32. Encyclopædia Britannica, inc. (n.d.). Occupation of Japan. Encyclopædia Britannica. Retrieved April 16, 2020, from https://www.britannica.com/event/occupation-of-Japan.
33. History.com Editors. (2009, October 29). Vietnam war. History.com. Retrieved February 18, 2020, from https://www.history.com/topics/vietnam-war/vietnam-war-history.]
34. Santa Barbara, J. (2006, December). Impact of war on children and imperative to end war. Croatian medical journal. Retrieved June 18, 2020, from https://www.ncbi.nlm.nih.gov/pmc/articles/PMC2080482/.

35. Deutsche Welle. (2017, February 11). German 'Wolf Children': The forgotten orphans of WWII. DW.COM. Retrieved June 6, 2020, from https://www.dw.com/en/german-wolf-children-the-forgotten-orphans-of-wwii/a-41214994#:~:text=Some%20say%20there%20were%20up,Prussia%20and%20Lithuania%20after%201945.
36. Deutsche Welle. (2015, July 16). What Germany's Post War refugees taught us about Integration. DW.COM. Retrieved June 6, 2020, from https://www.dw.com/en/what-germanys-postwar-refugees-taught-us-about-integration/a-18575558.
37. Migrant and displaced children. UNICEF. (2020, September). Retrieved October 15, 2020, from https://www.unicef.org/migrant-refugee-internally-displaced-children.
38. Arbatov, A. (n.d.). Nuclear deterrence: A guarantee or threat to strategic stability? Carnegie Moscow Center. Retrieved September 3, 2020, from https://carnegie.ru/2019/03/22/nuclear-deterrence-guarantee-or-threat-to-strategic-stability-pub-78663.
39. Vishwasrao, S., Schneider, M., & Chiang, E. P. (2018, November 23). The effects of military occupation on growth. Wiley Online Library. Retrieved January 4, 2020, from https://onlinelibrary.wiley.com/doi/epdf/10.1111/kykl.12194.
40. Strauss, W., & Howe, N. (1997). *The Fourth Turning: an American prophecy*. New York: Broadway Books.
41. "Young People & Tobacco." Action on Smoking and Health, https://ash.org.uk/category/information-and-resources/young-people-tobacco-information-and-resources/.
42. "Obesity in Children." UCSF Benioff Children's Hospital, https://www.ucsfbenioffchildrens.org/conditions/obesity#:~:text=A%20child%20with%20one%20obese,gain%20varies%20for%20dif-ferent%20people.
43. Sathya, Anup. "What Happens If You Have Affluent Parents?" Medium, Thrive Global, 1 Nov. 2018, https://medium.com/thrive-global/what-happens-if-you-have-affluent-parents-13c26f9f9a08.
44. Weiss, D. (n.d.). Cuneiform Letters. Archaeology Magazine. Retrieved February 9, 2020, from https://www.archaeology.org/issues/214-features/cuneiform/4368-cuneiform-letters.
45. Aesop. (n.d.). The bundle of sticks. Library of Congress Aesop Fables. Retrieved April 17, 2021, from http://read.gov/aesop/040.html.

46. Scott, Thomas L. (December 23, 2014). "9 of the Biggest Slave Owners in American History". Atlanta Black Star.
47. Byron, M. A. (2016, August 26). Aiken, William Jr.. South Carolina Encyclopedia. Retrieved November 13, 2020, from https://www.scencyclopedia.org/sce/entries/aiken-william-jr/.
48. https://www.inc.com/magazine/201511/paul-keegan/does-more-pay-mean-more-growth.html
49. shortbaldman. (2015, September 17.) What is the most important thing we have learned from the past? Reddit. Retrieved November 8, 2020, from https://www.reddit.com/r/history/comments/3ldqhh/what_is_the_most_important_thing_we_have_learned/.
50. Do you really get sick from being cold? UnityPoint Health. (n.d.). Retrieved November 24, 2020, from https://www.unitypoint.org/livewell/article.aspx?id=9161c3a0-54dc-46d7-a633-e1d15a5227e2.
51. Mosher, D. (2016, January 30). 101 things you thought were true but have actually been debunked by Science. Business Insider. Retrieved October 18, 2020, from https://www.businessinsider.com/worst-science-health-myths-2016-1#myth-milk-does-a-body-good-4.
52. Iftikhar, N. (2020, May 11). Is milk bad for you? Here's what the research says. Healthline. Retrieved October 24, 2020, from https://www.healthline.com/health/is-milk-bad-for-you#side-effects.
53. Grass is Greener (2019). 1h 37min | Documentary | 20 April 2019 (USA)
54. Smith, L. (2018, February 28). How a racist hate-monger masterminded America's war on drugs. Medium. Retrieved August 24, 2020, from https://timeline.com/harry-anslinger-racist-war-on-drugs-prison-industrial-complex-fb5cbc281189.
55. Nyamhistorymed. (2014, May 8). LaGuardia report. Books, Health and History. Retrieved August 19, 2020, from https://nyamcenterforhistory.org/tag/laguardia-report/.
56. Glenn, J. (1994). Fable of the Eagle and the Chicken. In Walk tall, you're a daughter of God (pp. 22-24). Salt Lake City, UT: Deseret Book. doi:http://www.greatexpectations.org/wp-content/uploads/pdf/exp4/FableoftheEagleandtheChicken.pdf
57. J.M.K.C. Donev et al. (2020). Energy Education - Energy [Online]. Available: https://energyeducation.ca/encyclopedia/Energy. [Accessed: December 21, 2020].
58. Clason, George S. (1955). The Richest Man in Babylon. New York: Hawthorn.

59. Proctor, B. (2018, January 16). How the Law of Attraction Works. Retrieved December 21, 2020, from https://www.proctorgallagherinstitute.com/6809/how-the-law-of-attraction-works
60. J. R. (2017, June 21). How to Take Charge of Your Life - Jim Rohn Personal Development. Retrieved December 01, 2020, from https://www.youtube.com/watch?v=DGIjuVbGP_A

About K. R. Hawthorne

I am an American writer born in Columbus, Ohio. The idea to write this book has swirled around in my head for years and I am elated that it is finally printed. I started my career in the fashion industry and transitioned into Human Resources and Entrepreneurship. If I have any advice for my younger self it would be to write the vision down for your life on paper. Follow that vision all the way through even when it gets hard. This is my first piece of literature and I hope that it incites new thoughts and actions in you the reader.

I currently live in Chicago, Illinois with my husband.

www.ingramcontent.com/pod-product-compliance
Lightning Source LLC
Chambersburg PA
CBHW030303100526
44590CB00012B/498